50 Hikes in the White Mountains

50 *Hikes*

In the White Mountains

Hikes and Backpacking Trips in the High Peaks Region of New Hampshire

Seventh Edition

DANIEL DOAN AND RUTH DOAN MACDOUGALL

THE COUNTRYMAN PRESS
Woodstock, Vermont

AN INVITATION TO THE READER

Developments, logging, and fires all take their toll on hiking trails, often from one year to the next. If you find that conditions along these 50 hikes have changed, please let the publisher know, so that corrections can be made in future editions. Address all correspondence to:

Editor, 50 Hikes Series
The Countryman Press
P.O. Box 748
Woodstock, VT 05091

Copyright © 1973, 1977, 1983, 1990 by Daniel Doan
Copyright © 1997, 2004, 2013 by Daniel Doan and Ruth Doan MacDougall
Seventh Edition

Explorer's Guide 50 Hikes in the White Mountains
978-1-58157-155-4

Book design by Glenn Suokko
Text composition by PerfecType, Nashville, TN
Maps by Erin Greb Cartography
© The Countryman Press
Interior photographs by Robert J. Kozlow unless otherwise noted
Frontispiece photograph: Pemigewasset Wilderness from Mount Lincoln by Robert J. Kozlow

Published by The Countryman Press,
P.O. Box 748, Woodstock, VT 05091
Distributed by W. W. Norton & Company, Inc.,
500 Fifth Avenue, New York, NY 10110
Printed in the United States of America

10 9 8 7 6 5 4 3 2 1

Acknowledgments

Thanks to all who have helped keep these hikes updated, especially the following:

Donald K. MacDougall
Marjorie M. Doan
Penelope Doan
Thane Joyal
James P. Gibbs
Hamish Gibbs
Kirk Dougal
Steven D. Smith
Hal and Peggy Graham of Trailwrights
Jason Berard
James Munroe
The Dartmouth Outing Club
Amy Gumprecht
Mary L. Kibling
The Over the Hill Hikers of Sandwich, NH
The Appalachian Mountain Club and the
U.S. Forest Service

Trying to analyze what he did when he went through the woods, he discovered that there were many little tricks to make it easier. He'd never thought about it before. You didn't watch your feet, but looked beyond and remembered the branches and rocks in the way. You timed your pace until you knew almost without glancing down what was in front of you while your eyes moved on ahead. You kept in mind the sun, when it showed through the clouds, and the sound of the brook. You used your hands to fend aside the branches and you balanced easy on your feet to suit the roughness of the ground and twisted your shoulders to slip around the trees.

—Daniel Doan,
Amos Jackman

50 Hikes in the White Mountains at a Glance

HIKE	DISTANCE (in miles)
1. Sabbaday Falls	1
2. West Rattlesnake Mountain	2
3. Boulder Loop	3.25
4. Kedron Flume	2
5. Three Ponds – Brown Brook Loop	5.5
6. East Pond	3
7. Greeley Ponds	4
8. Old Mast Road & Kelley Trail	5
9. Belknap Mountain	2
10. Mount Katherine	3.25
11. Mount Major	3
12. Hedgehog Mountain	5
13. Stinson Mountain	3.5
14. Mount Cardigan	3.5
15. Smarts Mountain	6.5
16. Artist's Bluff & Bald Mountain	1.5
17. Mount Pemigewasset	3.5
18. Basin-Cascades Trail	2.5
19. Lonesome Lake	3.25
20. Mount Flume	10
21. Mount Liberty	7.5
22. Mount Lincoln	8
23. Mount Lafayette	7.75
24. North Lafayette	9
25. Cannon Mountain	7.5

RISE IN FEET	VIEWS	GOOD FOR KIDS	WATERFALLS	NOTES
100		★	★	Simple & lovely
460	★	★		Lakes Region view
950	★	★		Keyed to educational stops
700	★	★	★	Rugged mountain fastness
500		★	★	Fine for gaining woods experience
780		★		Can include Little East Pond
400		★		Perfect for picnics
1,000		★	★	Woods walk & rock scramble
740	★	★		Blueberries!
250	★	★		A beautiful intervale
1,150	★	★		Stone hut ruins on summit
1,350	★	★		Vistas from ledges
1,400	★	★		Especially fine in October
1,300	★	★		Distinctive rock dome
1,900	★	★		The Daniel Doan Trail
600	★	★		Get a hiker's perspective
1,250	★	★		The Indian Head
550		★	★	Woods, falls, rock formations
1,000	★	★		Mountain lake in spectacular setting
3,367	★		★	Rock slides & exposed ledges
3,100	★			Stepped rock summit
3,350	★		★	Can include Mount Lafayette
3,400	★			Highest peak in Franconia Range
3,360	★			Remote from the crowd
2,100	★	?		Hiking alternative to tramway

50 Hikes in the White Mountains at a Glance

HIKE	DISTANCE (in miles)
26. Kinsman Mountain	10
27. Mount Moosilauke	7.5
28. Mount Garfield	10
29. Mount Osceola	6.5
30. Mount Tripyramid	11
31. Between the Notches: Zeacliff	8
32. Pinkham Notch: Crew-Cut Trail	2.25
33. Low's Bald Spot	4.25
34. Glen Boulder	3.25
35. Tuckerman Ravine	6.25
36. Mount Washington	9.25
37. The Alpine Garden	8.5
38. Mount Jefferson	5
39. Mount Adams	9
40. Mount Madison	10.5
41. Mount Kearsarge North	6.25
42. Tom-Field-Avalon Loop	8
43. Mount Starr King/Mount Waumbek	7.5
44. Mount Eisenhower	6.5
45. Mount Crawford	5
46. Mount Hancock	9.5
47. Sandwich Mountain	13
48. East Branch Region/Mount Carrigain	28
49. Mount Isolation	14
50. Mahoosuc Range	33

RISE IN FEET	VIEWS	GOOD FOR KIDS	WATERFALLS	NOTES
3,400	★			Two summits
2,500	★	?		"Dartmouth's Mountain"
3,050	★	?		Logging history
2,050	★			Highest of Waterville Valley Mountains
3,000	★			Three peaks & two slides!
1,500	★	★	★	Pemigewasset Wilderness views
400	★	★		Introduction to Pinkham
1,050	★	★		Experience Mount Washington
1,750	★	?	★	A landmark
2,500	★	?	★	To the Snow Arch
3,800	★		★	The western approach
3,500	★			Flowers: mid-June to July
2,700	★			Memorable ledges: the Caps
4,500	★			Second in height to Mount Washington
3,800	★		★	End of Presidential Range
2,600	★	?		New Hampshire & Maine views
2,800	★		★	Three summits
2,600	★	?		See the Presidentials from the north
2,750	★	?		Great trail construction
2,100	★	★		Historic & rewarding hike
2,400	★	★		Test yourself gently
2,500	★	★	★	Camp at Black Mountain Pond
3,300	★		★	Pemigewasset Wilderness
3,200	★			A remote peak
8,600	★		★	A weeklong adventure

Contents

MOUNT WASHINGTON REGION

BACKPACKING HIKES

Preface to the Seventh Edition

In August 2011, in the Mead Conservation Center at the foot of Mount Israel in Center Sandwich, New Hampshire, the New Hampshire Writers' Project held a workshop-celebration of the hundredth birthday of the Weeks Act, which created the White Mountain National Forest. My niece, Thane Joyal, and I were invited to talk about Dan Doan, her grandfather and my father. Thane's son, Hamish Gibbs, then fifteen years old, also took part in this "Appreciation of Daniel Doan."

My sister, Penelope, and I grew up hiking with Dan. Thane became the next generation to do so. Dan died before Hamish was born, but Hamish has grown up hiking with his parents. In the years since Dan's death in 1993, we have all been involved in keeping Dan's books updated, checking trails with his books in our hands.

At the workshop, Thane spoke about this and about growing up in a family that took writing as well as hiking for granted.

I described Dan's background. His roots were in Orford, New Hampshire, where his maternal grandmother was born. His father was a Unitarian minister, and the family lived in other states, but, as Dan wrote, "Orford had been a constant in my life because our house there was my summer home all through my boyhood. Aunts, uncles, and cousins near or distant lived there summers or year-round. Falling in love with a locality can be as powerful an emotion as falling in love with a person. In some form it lasts a lifetime."

It was here that Dan began exploring the woods and first climbed Mount Cube (see *50 More Hikes in New Hampshire*) and Smarts Mountain (see Hike 15 in this book for a day hike and *50 More Hikes in New Hampshire* for a backpacking hike).

Then in 1929, two years after his father died in Winchester, Massachusetts, Dan moved with his mother to Hanover and thus at age fifteen came to live permanently in New Hampshire. After he graduated from Dartmouth, he and my mother, Ernestine, set up housekeeping on a chicken farm in Orfordville. After this they bought a chicken farm in Belmont, where Penny and I were born.

Dan's plan was to earn a living by farming and by writing short stories. In those days, magazines published a lot of stories and paid well for them. Dan later commented, his tone ironic, "I even thought the plan was sound." The eggs sold, and some of the stories sold, but it wasn't enough to support the family. So after Penny was born we moved to Laconia, and Dan went to work at a manufacturing company, Scott & Williams.

He had given up farming, but he didn't give up writing. His first novel, *The Crystal Years*, was published in 1952. It's a coming-of-age tale about a boy who moves from Boston to New Hampshire. *Amos Jackman*, published in 1957, was inspired by the town of Quinttown, whose abandoned farmland he had discovered while fishing near Smarts Mountain.

After retiring at age 51, Dan taught briefly at the short-lived Gunstock College in Laconia and devoted himself to writing and hiking—and writing *about* hiking. The result was the two hiking books that have become classics: the one you're reading and its sequel, *50 More.*

He also wrote a history of New Hampshire's North Country, called *Indian Stream Republic: Settling a New England Frontier, 1785–1842.* This was published posthumously in 1997.

In 1982 my mother died. Dan married Marjorie, a hiking friend, and they moved to Jefferson, New Hampshire. There Dan wrote *Our Last Backpack,* about a weeklong hike in the Mahoosucs (see Hike 50 in this book). It's a memoir that encompasses the history of New Hampshire's mountains and the personal history of two old friends who had hiked together since they were boys in Orford. The book was published just before his death.

By then, I had been helping him keep his hiking books updated. Ever since I had given him my first story at age six, we had been in the same business, so to speak, sharing the love of writing. He knew that I would take over the books after he died.

A few months before his death, the Dartmouth Outing Club named a Smarts Mountain trail the Daniel Doan Trail (see Hike 15). A year after his death I accepted for him the New Hampshire Writers' Project's Lifetime Achievement Award.

And now Thane and I were at this NHWP celebration, talking about Dan Doan.

As I explained to the writers there, updating the hiking books had, in addition to the usual challenges such as writing trailhead directions and trail descriptions, a unique challenge: voice. Dan and I shared what I thought of as a family voice, similar choices of words and turns of phrase. I hoped that I could slip mine into the text without jarring as I added updates and that when I wrote an entirely new hike it would be a form of harmonizing.

Thane and Hamish   JAMES P. GIBBS

Some thoughts about equipment. I've mentioned in previous editions that besides the items Dan lists in the Clothing and Equipment section of the Introduction, my pack contains, for a day hike, an extra pair of socks, a bandanna, a small flashlight, a small first-aid kit, a whistle, sunglasses, sunscreen, lip balm, notebook and pencil, and a plastic trash bag for a variety of purposes, including having a tarp to sit on. Nowadays I carry a cell phone and use trekking poles.

Food, of course, is a very important item in the pack. Dan advises bringing extra, just in case. As I'm putting it all into my lunch bag I think ahead to lunch on the trail and remember how a hiking friend once remarked as we sat on a summit and he opened his lunch bag, "You know why I hike? Peanut-butter-and-jelly sandwiches."

—Ruth Doan MacDougall
2013

Introduction

These excursions into New Hampshire's White Mountains are intended to initiate the beginner and entertain the experienced hiker. There are 45 day hikes and five overnight backpacking hikes. They are arranged from short to long and from gradual to steep. The first four hikes are suitable for family outings. Then there are four woods walks, seven hikes in small mountains, and 30 hikes in and around the Franconia Range and the Presidential Range. The five backpacking hikes run from a weekend to a week. Some of the hikes loop around to their starting points, which are, of course, the places where you leave your car. Other hikes follow the same route up to their destinations and back.

Most of the hikes are within the central White Mountains. Several take you to lesser-known outlying summits. The corners of the hiking territory are: Mount Major (Hike 11), southeast near Lake Winnipesaukee; Mount Cardigan (Hike 14), southwest near Canaan; Mount Starr King (Hike 43), northwest in Jefferson; and Old Speck Mountain (Hike 50), northeast at Grafton Notch, Maine. Within this area, the hikes take you up all the major peaks of the White Mountains. The map facing the contents page clearly shows the location of each hike.

The White Mountain hiking season extends from May into October. Winter weather occurs early and late. Above treeline, you may encounter icy storms at any time, even during the season. June and July have their blackflies and mosquitoes; you'll need insect repellent. To my mind, September is the best hiking month. The heat of July, the August haze, and the bugs are gone for the season. Cool air and clear skies offset the customary September storms.

THE TRAILS

The hikes follow established, well-marked trails maintained by the U.S. Forest Service, the New Hampshire Division of Parks and Recreation, the Appalachian Mountain Club (AMC), and various other clubs. Forty-five of the hikes are in the White Mountain National Forest or in nearby state reservations. Some of the hikes begin on, or cross, private land owned by lumber companies, Dartmouth College, or others. On trails crossing boundaries between private land and the national forest, the forest service posts small signs at the boundaries. Any abuse of the privilege granted to hikers on this private land could result in NO TRESPASSING signs.

The mountain trails change due to slides, washouts, new beaver ponds, trees downed by winds, and heavy use. On the other hand, some, like the Crawford Path, have hardly changed in nearly 200 years. When necessary, trails, or sections of them, are relocated. Access roads and parking places may be restricted or relocated. For the latest information, check with the U.S. Forest Service, the Appalachian Mountain Club, or the New Hampshire Department of Resources and Economic Development. Web sites for these and other organizations are listed under "Addresses" at the end of this Introduction.

The composite maps, featuring topographic base maps with the described hiking route superimposed on them, allow the hiker to appraise the terrain and to gauge hiking difficulty and distance. These maps use portions of both United States Geological Survey (USGS) and Forest Service (USDA) quadrangles. The latter are of more recent vintage and are therefore more up-to-date in terms of trails, roads, and other man-made features. Both use the USGS contour base. Road and trail numbers on the forest service quads are for administrative purposes and are of no particular consequence to hikers. The USGS maps are available in a variety of retail outlets as well as directly from the USGS Web site, where you can also buy CD-ROMs. At the National Geographic Web site you can buy two National Geographic Trails Illustrated Maps of this area, #740: Franconia Notch/North Conway, and #741: Presidential Range/Gorham. Any serious hiker should also be equipped with the *AMC White Mountain Guide* and the excellent maps that come with it. The AMC maps are kept as modern as possible by reissues with each edition of the *Guide.* The most accurate map of all for a portion of the White Mountains is Brad Washburn's *Mount Washington and the Heart of the Presidential Range,* also published by the AMC. The *AMC White Mountain Guide* and Washburn's Mount Washington map may be purchased at Pinkham Notch Visitor Center and at sporting goods stores, outfitters, bookstores throughout New Hampshire, and online. The *White Mountain Guide* includes only paper maps, but Tyvek weatherproof maps can be bought separately.

LOGGING ROADS

The descriptions of the hikes refer often to logging roads. Almost all of these are *old* logging roads that have become part of the new forests. They are not raw bulldozed cuts for heavy modern logging machines. Only the trails keep them open. The old roads were graded for horses and sleds; although plentifully strewn with rocks, they follow the slopes at gentle angles. Together with the former railroad grades along the valleys, these old logging roads provide the best walking in the mountains.

The present logging operations supervised by the forest service usually leave the trails in wooded corridors. When you look off from various summits, you will see the clearcuts as irregular squares or rectangles of slash or sprouts.

The Pemigewasset Wilderness, whose mountains and rivers are drained by the East Branch of the Pemigewasset River, is a fascinating former logging territory, and a splendid example of new forests on land once devastated by logging and fires. Now officially a wilderness, it contains a network of trails connecting with the main Wilderness Trail, which in turn connects with the Kancamagus Highway by way of the Lincoln Woods Trail.

DISTANCE, WALKING TIME, AND VERTICAL RISE

Each hike description begins with figures for distance, walking time, and vertical rise. These are gauges by which you can evaluate the hikes.

The times allow for leisurely climbing, which seems to me the only pleasant and sensible way, but they do not include rest periods, lunch breaks, view-gazing, or bird-watching. Young, hardy climbers may be able to cut the times in half.

The vertical-rise figure tells you the approximate distance up. If you start at a 1,000-foot elevation and climb to a 2,500-foot summit, you may walk 2 miles or 5, but your vertical rise is 1,500 feet. Sometimes you climb down into a valley and up again to a summit; your return trip will thus involve some climbing, which is included in the total, or round-trip, vertical-rise figure. As a general rule, the greater the vertical rise per mile, the more strenuous the climb.

THE WHITE MOUNTAIN NATIONAL FOREST

The State of New Hampshire had disposed of its public land by the mid-1800s, and logging began in earnest after the Civil War. Men with axes felled trees throughout the North Country—except in the White Mountains' most remote valleys, where the steep slopes presented transportation problems. The rivers were too shallow and rocky for log drives.

Because of this and other difficulties, the forests of red spruce, pine, hemlock, and cedar in the White Mountains remained standing until late in the era, and some were bypassed completely as lumbermen cut a swath from Maine to Minnesota.

Finally, railroads opened the valleys in the 1880s and 1890s, and much of the timber was cut by 1900. Logging continued through the First World War and even as late as the 1930s, but, long before the cutting was complete, forest fires had devastated large tracts of cut-over land.

Conservationists, led primarily by the Society for the Protection of New Hampshire Forests, came to the rescue of the White Mountains in the early 1900s. The federal government purchased areas for watershed protection under the Weeks Act beginning in 1912. The White Mountain National Forest now covers more than 790,000 acres, a portion of which extends into Maine.

The land is managed by the U.S. Forest Service under directives based on "multiple use." Among these uses are timber production, watershed protection, recreation development, and wildlife protection. Nine Scenic Areas have been designated by the forest service: Gibbs Brook, Greeley Ponds, Pinkham Notch, Lafayette Brook, Rocky Gorge, Lincoln Woods, Sawyer Pond, Mount Chocorua, Snyder Brook. Three Research Natural Areas include The Bowl, the Alpine Garden, and Nancy Brook. In addition, there are six Wilderness Areas mandated by Congress: Great Gulf, Presidential–Dry River (both on Mount Washington), Pemigewasset, Sandwich Range, Caribou–Speckled Mountain, and Wild River. These Wilderness Areas preserve a total of 149,500 acres of valleys, ponds, and mountains in their natural beauty.

Ruth's Note: Parking passes are now required where signs designate fee areas. These passes can be purchased at the White Mountain National Forest headquarters in Campton, at ranger stations, visitors centers, local businesses, at the AMC information centers in Crawford Notch and Pinkham Notch, and online. There are also self-service fee-collection tubes installed at various trailhead parking areas. For more information, see the White Mountain National Forest Web site.

TREES AND ANIMALS

The mountainsides are now covered by hardwood forests of beech, maple, yellow birch, and white birch, which took over after the destruction of the spruce. Evergreens remain predominant in the swamps. The upper summits, from about 3,000 feet to treeline, are spruce/fir forests interspersed with white birch and mountain ash.

You will probably meet no dangerous animal life. This is not rattlesnake country. Black bears and wildcats are shy. I recall only six bears in 55 years of walking the mountains, and they were all going away fast when they became aware of me.

Ruth's Note: If you encounter a bear on the trail, the New Hampshire Fish and Game Department advises you to keep your distance and make noise–talking, clapping, singing–to let it know you're there. If it tries a "bluff charge," don't run; maintain eye contact and slowly back away. Whether or not to drop your pack (with its tantalizing food) is a matter of debate, for such an action may encourage a bear to associate a hiker with food, but if necessary, abandon the pack and worry about ethics later. At campsites, bears can be a problem, so take careful precautions not to attract them. Do your cooking at least 100 feet downwind of the campsite, and keep your food and cooking utensils separate from your sleeping area. Put food scraps in closed containers. Hang the food at least 10 feet off the ground and 5 feet out on a limb that won't support a bear.

Porcupines can be dangerous to an aggressive dog; otherwise they mind their own business. Even *Homo sapiens* seems gentler in the mountains.

White-tailed deer are forest denizens seldom seen in the higher mountains. You probably won't see one of the eastern coyotes now roaming the region; they survive by avoiding people, and have been doing so successfully since their arrival in the 1970s. You may see a moose. They have become much more common; you'll certainly see their oxlike tracks. (Ruth's Note: If you do see a moose, admire from afar. Moose can be unpredictable and aggressive. If a moose charges, the advice is to run like hell. Also, when you're driving to and from a trailhead, keep an eye out for moose. There are many car-moose collisions, as the "Brake for Moose" highway signs and bumper stickers warn).

Fishers, otters, mink, and weasels are not often seen. You'll probably see a snowshoe rabbit flash quickly into cover. Red squirrels and chipmunks will chatter at you. Coons, skunks, foxes, and flying squirrels come out at night.

In the text I mention birds because I like to watch them. (Ravens are common now but were not when I first described the hikes in 1973.) Trees, flowers, and plants mean more if you know their names. Field guides to identify vegetation, birds, and animals will increase your enjoyment.

CLOTHING AND EQUIPMENT

Careful consideration and selection of the clothing and equipment for your hikes are essential. Basic apparel includes a shirt, walking pants or shorts (avoid cotton, which gets cold when wet, and try cotton-synthetic blends or entirely synthetic material), comfortable underwear, and hiking boots and socks.

I recommend modern lightweight hiking boots. They are based on designs and materials from jogging shoes. During a long hike in these boots you can avoid lifting a ton or more of the boot-weight required if you had worn a pair of clumpers. I wear canvas and leather boots with a relatively thin lug sole, about 2 pounds. For backpacking, you need the protection of a more conventional leather boot. Break in your boots completely before you commit your feet to a long hike in them. This applies to both standard leather boots and the lightweights. Heavy mountaineering boots are unnecessary for the hikes in this book.

As for socks, one pair of sock liners under one pair of lightweight wool or synthetic-blend socks seems to be the best combination.

As long as the weather is fair, the above clothing is all you'll need to wear. Pack the rest of your equipment and spare clothes in a strong, waterproof knapsack, usually called a "day pack." Don't dangle equipment from belt or shoulder straps. No bulging pockets. Here's what you'll need to pack: heavy wool shirt or sweater (wool stays warm when wet),

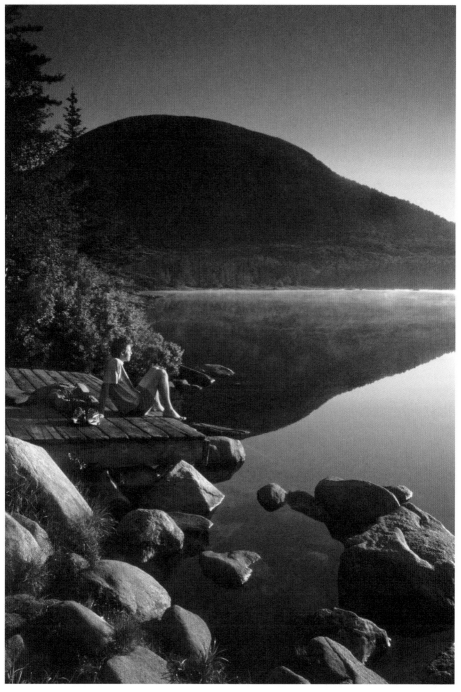

Lonesome Lake

or a synthetic fleece or insulated jacket; poncho or rain suit with hood; nylon parka or shell; hat; gloves; warm pants; matches and firestarter in a waterproof container; compass; map and guidebook; pocketknife with can opener and screwdriver; insect repellent; two quarts of water in canteens or other containers; lunch; and spare food for two meals.

Consider buying a parka made of one of the laminated materials that are microporous, making them both breathable and waterproof. There are many such parkas in a wide range of styles and uses. The materials are also used for rain pants and the uppers of boots. Though expensive, this type of clothing can eliminate your other rain gear for active, sweat-inducing exercise, but don't expect a miracle of total sweat evaporation. Such a parka can be substituted at times for a windproof shell.

I like a plastic transparent compass with movable base for setting a course. (Note: In the White Mountains, your compass points about 16 degrees west.) I also use plastic flask-shaped water bottles (1-pint size) instead of canteens.

If you're backpacking, you'll need everything on the day-hiker's list and more. In addition to an adequately large pack (too varied for discussion here), you'll want to take a tent, or at least a waterproof tarp; a hiker's gas stove, cook kit, forks and spoons; a sleeping bag in a stuff sack; a foam pad to place under your sleeping bag at night; a small first-aid kit, including moleskin for foot blisters (no snakebite kit necessary, but take insect repellent); soap and a towel; a small flashlight and perhaps a headlamp, two candles, and extra matches in a waterproof container; a small hatchet or saw (optional); 50 feet of light nylon cord for a variety of uses, including hanging food from trees out of reach of bears; and meals for each day of the

trip. Food should be light and easy to prepare. Include ready-to-eat food for lunches. Standard necessities can be found at your supermarket: oatmeal, sugar, dried milk, tea, salt, hard breads, cheese, canned meats, dried soups, etc. At your backpacking shop choose freeze-dried foods for super-light nourishment. (Ruth's Note: If you don't want to boil water, pack a filtration device or iodine treatment. See Dan's comments about giardia in the Safety section of this Introduction.)

Because equipment for backpacking is so extensive, and the choice arouses such vehement contention, you may want to read a book on the subject and explore a shop or catalog that specializes in backpacking and mountaineering equipment. If you are new to backpacking, I suggest you rent your pack, tent, and other gear for the first few trips to learn what you will want to buy. Whatever you finally decide to take, be sure to set everything up at home and try it out before heading into the mountains.

Equipment is no substitute for experience. Learning how to walk in the woods is more important than the best hiking boots money can buy.

RULES AND REGULATIONS

All rules and guidelines for hikers in the White Mountains, both those of the forest service and those promoted by the Appalachian Mountain Club, have been developed to save the forest from its greatest enemy, fire, and to preserve areas that are becoming more and more popular, especially those with delicate ecology near treeline and above in the alpine zone. The days of the roaring campfire and the woodsman's bough bed are over.

The rules apply mostly to campers and backpackers, rather than day hikers. Common sense and thoughtful consideration of others will go far to direct your behavior into conformation with rules, but there are some regulations you should know about. Hikers on private property cannot legally build wood or charcoal fires without the landowner's permission and a fire permit from the district fire chief. Use a portable stove. No overnight camping is allowed on private property without the landowner's permission. Carry out all your trash. Don't cut trees or boughs or destroy plants. Park your car well off roads. Don't park in any opening into the woods no matter how ancient, and of course never in any logging road or in front of a gate. A state law prohibits obstruction of a right-of-way.

For the White Mountain National Forest, the long-standing requirement of fire permits was discontinued in 1985. There are, however, special regulations about camping and fires. You should get the latest seasonal information from the ranger stations or visitors centers.

The AMC offers information at Pinkham Notch Visitor Center and at the Crawford Depot in Crawford Notch.

The State of New Hampshire has rules for its parks, reservations, and forests. In general, no camping or wood or charcoal fires are allowed outside designated campgrounds and picnic areas. Regulations are posted. Check the NH Division of Parks and Recreation Web site.

Although in the White Mountain National Forest fire permits are no longer required, you must obtain and abide by the forest service publication "Backcountry Camping Rules," which provides detailed listings of current limitations on camping and fires. Where overuse has compacted the soil and damaged plants and trees, natural recovery is encouraged by Forest Protection Areas (formerly called Restricted Use Areas, or RUAs) and future harm is prevented. Check the latest regulations when you pick up the "Backcountry Camping Rules" at a ranger station or online, and

consult the White Mountain National Forest Web site for updates.

I cannot emphasize enough your obligation to stay on trails when you are above treeline. Fragile alpine plants are at the mercy of hiking boots and once damaged may never recover. The mountains and your fellow hikers deserve an uncluttered trail. No litter, no trash left behind. And no random elimination—to put it politely, copy the cat, and make sure you're 100 long paces away from any trail, stream, pond, or spring. No candy wrappers, cans, or any of the slick packaging our civilization provides us for throwing away. If you take them in, take them out again in your pack. The motto is: "Carry in and carry out!" And another: "Leave no trace."

HUTS AND SHELTERS

In the White Mountains the Appalachian Mountain Club and the U.S. Forest Service maintain most of the trails and shelters.

Long a prime mover in this area, the AMC was founded in 1876. It maintains more than 1,400 miles of trails, as well as shelters and mountain huts. At its eight huts, crews provide meals and lodging for hikers during the summer. In the spring, some huts have self-service accommodations (carry your own food and equipment); three of the huts are open through the winter on a self-service basis. Check the AMC Web site for more information about rates and reservations.

The AMC Pinkham Notch Visitor Center on NH 16 is open year-round to accommodate skiers and hikers, and it also serves as headquarters for the system of trails, shelters, and huts. The AMC's Highland Center in Crawford Notch offers lodging, educational programs, workshops, and skills training.

A note on winter excursions: Snowshoes and cross-country skis can extend your season to almost 12 months. Both sports are fascinating but require knowledge and experience for full enjoyment and safety.

PHYSICAL FITNESS

Good physical condition increases hiking pleasure. Without it, the more strenuous hikes are no pleasure at all, and there may be harm and danger.

If you wait until warm weather to get in shape, the arrangement of hikes in this book will break the news to your body that you're going to take it walking. Nobody has to be an athlete to succeed with Hike 1; Mount Washington is something else again. In preparation for the longer climbs in the high Franconias and Presidentials, I've included a few relatively easy hikes for each region. In the Franconia Region, they are numbers 16, 17, 18, and 19. In the Presidentials, they are numbers 32, 33, 34, and 35.

Stamina developed for walking and climbing provides not only pleasure but also an important safety margin in the mountains. It's a form of insurance you can take out yourself.

SAFETY

Almost every year, the mountains claim at least one hiker's life. Storms are sudden and fierce above treeline. Trails over the bare rocks, marked only by cairns and signs at the junctions, disappear in the clouds and wind-driven rain, sleet, and snow. Electrical storms shoot down lightning that bounces from the rocks amid the torrential rain. Besides physical fitness, two precautions may help you survive these dangers. First, in the face of threatening weather forecasts, don't go mountain climbing, or go to some lesser peak or a woods trail. Second, in the face of gathering low clouds and wind at treeline, turn back. The woods and shelter are only a few steps behind you; ahead you will climb into increasingly thick fog and winds so strong you'll be unable to stand.

On many trails leading above treeline, a forest service sign will warn you of the dangers ahead. They aren't kidding, either; above treeline you're in hazardous territory. Perhaps this fact, along with the tremendous views and the thrill of being there on your own two feet, gives above-treeline hiking its excitement.

It's important to hike with a companion. (Two old friends hike best together; I've been lucky this way.) Stay together. This is a rule of every mountain clubber, experienced climber, and all officials delegated to find the lost or injured lone hiker.

Carry a compass. Carry a map that you have studied so you know about the route and the trails. (Ruth's Note: If you use a GPS device, remember its limitations. The same goes for Personal Locator Beacons and cell phones. For more information about safety in general, see www.hikesafe.com.)

Be prepared to spend a night out in the woods or under a rock. This means carrying extra food, water, warm clothing, and waterproof outerwear in a knapsack.

Purity of drinking water cannot be assumed just because a stream is clear and cold and tumbling down a sylvan valley. It might contain Giardia lamblia, a common intestinal parasite, which causes delayed diarrhea, cramps, loss of appetite and weight, as well as other unpleasant symptoms. Among animals other than humans, beavers are likely to infect streams and ponds in the mountains. Boiling, filtration, and chemical treatment are now standard preventive measures. Note that my mention of water in these hikes does not mean safe water.

And last of all—but so important it might be first—before you set out, tell someone where you're going, and give an alternate place for bad weather. Then go there, one or the other, and enjoy yourself. The hike is supposed to be fun. No bitching: not about the trail, the weather, or the world. Leave that attitude back with "civilization" and your other troubles.

I wish you years and years of great hikes in the White Mountains of New Hampshire.

Ruth's Note: In May 2003, the most popular sight in the White Mountains disappeared when a famous granite formation known as the Old Man of the Mountain collapsed. New Hampshire's state symbol, it had watched over Franconia Notch for eons. As I look at a paperweight my mother made from a photograph my father took of my sister and me posing with the Old Man in the background, I think how many other such photos have been snapped over the years and how many other people cherish memories of the Old Man. My favorite memory of all is the fun my father had flying a kite off the Old Man's forehead.

ADDRESSES

Appalachian Mountain Club

5 Joy Street
Boston, Massachusetts 02108

or

Pinkham Notch Visitor Center
Gorham, New Hampshire 03581
www.outdoors.org

White Mountain National Forest

Supervisor's Office and Pemigewasset
   Ranger Station
Forest Headquarters
71 White Mountain Drive
Campton, NH 03223
603-536-6100
www.fs.usda.gov/whitemountain

New Hampshire Department of Resources and Economic Development

172 Pembroke Road
Concord, New Hampshire 03301
www.dred.state.nh.us

New Hampshire Division of Parks and Recreation

172 Pembroke Road
Concord, New Hampshire 03301
www.nhstateparks.org

Society for the Protection of New Hampshire Forests

54 Portsmouth Street
Concord, New Hampshire 03301
www.forestsociety.org

United States Geological Survey

Box 25286
Denver, Colorado 80225
www.usgs.gov

KEY TO MAP SYMBOLS

- ▬ ▬ ▬   main trail
- ● ● ●   side trail
- ⚡   Appalachian Trail
- ⛺   shelter
- Ⓟ   parking

Introductory Hikes

His senses seemed to expand and reach out toward the woods and hills around him, absorbing the pine smell, the green trees and blue sky, the soft earth, the muted bird calls and the breeze in the boughs. His senses focused all these things like a magnifying glass concentrating the sun's rays until he was on fire with joy.

–Daniel Doan,
The Crystal Years

1

Sabbaday Falls

Distance (picnic area to falls and back): 1 mile

Walking time: ½ hour

Vertical rise: 100 feet

Maps: USDA/FS 7½' Mt. Tripyramid; USGS 15' Mt. Chocorua

No more than an afternoon's jaunt, this popular short hike to Sabbaday Falls conveys an important message about the mountains. It suggests a new world to explore: one filled with outdoor sights, sounds, and sensations. It arouses a new or forgotten interest in the woods, the streams, and the miles of mountainous terrain around you.

HOW TO GET THERE

On NH 16 in Conway, turn onto the Kancamagus Highway (NH 112) and drive 15.7 miles to Sabbaday Falls Picnic Ground on the south side of the Kancamagus. If you are coming from the west, the picnic area is 20.4 miles from I-93 in Lincoln.

THE TRAIL

At the start of the Sabbaday Brook Trail, signs tell you about the history of the falls, and at the falls themselves you'll come to signs describing their geology.

The trail begins as a graded path in a forest of maple, beech, and birch leading up to the base of the ledges through which the stream cuts its way. A side trail, left, takes you down to the lower pool. Stone steps and peeled-log railings ease the way up the ledges above the narrow flume that was formed by water wearing away a basalt dike in surrounding granite. From a deep pothole, the stream pours down into the flume.

The walkway returns to the Sabbaday Brook Trail above the falls. (The Sabbaday Brook Trail continues up the brook toward Mount Tripyramid.) Take the trail back to your car.

Westward, the Kancamagus Highway rises steadily to Kancamagus Pass at 2,855 feet, then winds down to Lincoln and I-93 at North Woodstock. Signs mark other trails into the mountains north and south. (See hikes to Greeley Ponds, number 7, and Mount Hancock, number 46. Eastward are Hedgehog Mountain, number 12, and Boulder Loop, number 3.) Before driving the highway, check your car's gas gauge; there are no service stations on the 34.5 miles between Conway and Lincoln.

The adventure of driving the highway persists despite its popularity and the blacktop surface added in 1963. Before that, many tourists did not know of the completion of the gravel road's upper section, done in the summer of 1959, and uncertainty added spice. One tourist stopped near the Conway end to question an old lady rocking on her porch: "Does this road go across the mountains?" After a moment's thought she told him: "Well, a lot of cars pass by here and don't come back."

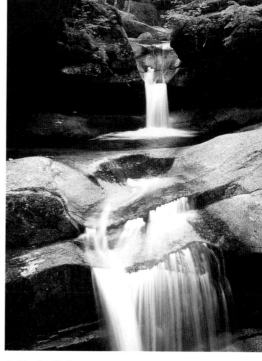

Sabbaday Falls   ROBERT J. KOZLOW

2

West Rattlesnake Mountain

Distance (round trip): 2 miles
Walking time: 1 hour
Vertical rise: 460 feet
Maps: USDA/FS 7½' Squam Mountains; USGS 7½' Squam Mountains

This hike delivers a lot of bang for the buck. An easy climb leads you to one of the most beautiful views in New Hampshire's Lakes Region.

At the summit of this 1,243-foot western peak of Rattlesnake Mountain, you look down on Squam Lake, its blue emphasized by the many green islands and the green shoreline curving around coves and inlets. The boats down there are as tiny as water bugs, scooting along leaving silent wakes.

In the distance you see more water, Lake Winnipesaukee, and mountains. Red Hill is nearest on the southeast, then there's Copple Crown, Belknap Mountain, Piper Mountain, and Mount Major, with Mount Kearsarge and Ragged Mountain to the southwest and Bridgewater Mountain and Hersey Mountain on the west.

Rattlesnake Mountain is often referred to as the Rattlesnakes to include the eastern peak. The original name of the mountain was Peaked Hill. Because New Hampshire's only rattlesnake, the timber rattlesnake, is rare, it's assumed that the Rattlesnake Mountain name came from a mix-up with the northern water snake.

The Squam Lakes Association, founded in 1904, maintains the trails in the Squam region and publishes a fine trail map. See www.squamlakes.org.

Rattlesnake Mountain is popular, and the Old Bridle Path is its most popular trail. Try to go on a weekday, not a weekend. The Squam Lakes Association asks that you keep your group size to six or less and hike in single file.

Introductory Hikes

HOW TO GET THERE

If you're coming from the south, turn off US 3 in Holderness onto NH 113, and drive 5.3 miles to the new parking area on the right.

From the north on NH 113, drive 6.3 miles from the overhead blinking light in Center Sandwich to the new parking area on the left.

THE TRAIL

The new start of the trail leaves the parking area at a kiosk and quickly joins the Old Bridle Path. You climb smoothly up this wide, leafy trail, old and new sections alternating. You can study the log stairs and waterbars that trail workers have built to combat erosion. Listen to the birdsong burbling. You might even hear a hermit thrush, the "American nightingale."

At a wide ledge near the top, bear left up the main trail. You'll soon come to the last flight of stairs.

Then—the famous view.

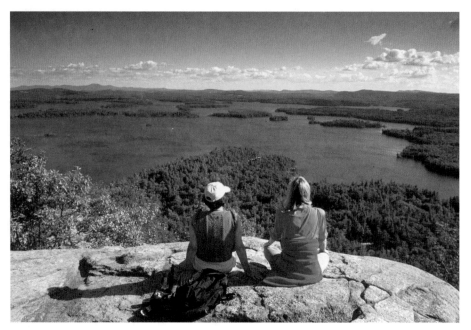

View from West Rattlesnake

ROBERT J. KOZLOW

Corral your kids. These ledges have dangerous drops, so everybody should stay well back from the edge.

Enjoy your picnic, the view, the breeze, and perhaps the sight of a hawk overhead. After, as you descend the Old Bridle Path, this introduction to Squam may have you planning a hike to East Rattlesnake on less-traveled trails and then explorations of nearby mountains. (See Mounts Morgan and Percival in *50 More Hikes in New Hampshire.*)

3

Boulder Loop

Distance (around the loop, including spur to ledges): 3¼ miles

Walking time: 3 hours

Vertical rise: 950 feet

Maps: USDA/FS 7½' North Conway West; USGS 15' North Conway

The Boulder Loop Trail is for family walking and enjoyment. It should be considered a climb rather than a picnic jaunt. Suitable hiking shoes and other clothing are necessary. A small knapsack frees your hands of lunch, camera, and jacket.

HOW TO GET THERE

Turn off NH 16 just west of Conway onto the Kancamagus Highway. Six miles from this junction, you'll see signs on the right for Passaconaway Road, the Covered Bridge Campground, and Boulder Loop. Turn right here and drive across the covered bridge over the Swift River. Turn right again and watch for the sign for Boulder Loop Trail parking.

THE TRAIL

From the parking area, cross the road to the trail, which soon forks. Bear left. You'll come to a rock, smoothed by the ages, extending 100 feet along the trail and reaching up 30 feet. Lichens grow on it much as they did when they were the first plants on the bare rock of the world.

Along the trail through hardwoods and evergreens, you see examples of soil formation and forest origins from the time of the glacier 50,000 years ago: erosion, lichens and moss, elementary plants and trees, mature specimens of oak, spruce, fir, pine, hemlock, beech, maple, birch, ash, and various other trees native to the White Mountains.

You also see boulders, a rock slide, a brook, blowdowns from a northeast storm, fracturing granite, dry slopes with plants adapted to that sunny environment, contrasting cool-moist slopes, and birds and flowers in season.

The trail takes you to a splendid outlook 1,000 feet above the Passaconaway Valley. A spur trail leads to ledges giving views from the highest elevation. You see Mount Chocorua's sharp peak and the bulky Mount Passaconaway beyond the nearer forested ridges. These lookoffs have the inherent dangers of all cliffs.

Descending through the hardwood forest on the return half of the loop, you pass tall beeches. Watch for claw marks on the smooth gray bark. Bears climb in the fall for beechnuts.

View from Boulder Loop   ROBERT J. KOZLOW

4

Kedron Flume

Distance (round trip): 2 miles

Walking time: 1¾ hours

Vertical rise: 700 feet

Maps: USDA/FS 7½' Crawford Notch; USGS 7½' Crawford Notch

Crawford Notch is a pass through the mountains. For years it provided a route between the interior Connecticut River valley and the seacoast region. Discovered by hunters in the days when New Hampshire was a royal province, and explored by settlers following the Saco River after the Revolution, Crawford Notch became a teamsters' passage between sheer cliffs and steep forested slopes. The notch is now a state park. A railroad and US 302 wind through it. But a short distance into the woods the mountains are still primitive and rugged.

HOW TO GET THERE

For a brief hike into this mountain fastness, take US 302 at the junction with US 3 in Twin Mountain, and drive about 11 miles through the notch's gateway crags to the parking area at the Willey House Historical Site. If you are coming from the east, drive about 18 miles on US 302 from the junction with NH 16 in Glen.

THE TRAIL

The Kedron Flume Trail is to the right of the picnic tables, which are tucked into the steep slope. You start climbing immediately, following blue blazes.

The trail leads you to the railroad track near the site of the earth avalanche that wiped out the Willey family in the summer of 1826. As you approach the track, you'll see a trestle culvert, with moss creeping over stones and mortar. This Maine Central Railroad track was abandoned in 1984. But in 1995 the Conway Scenic Railroad began

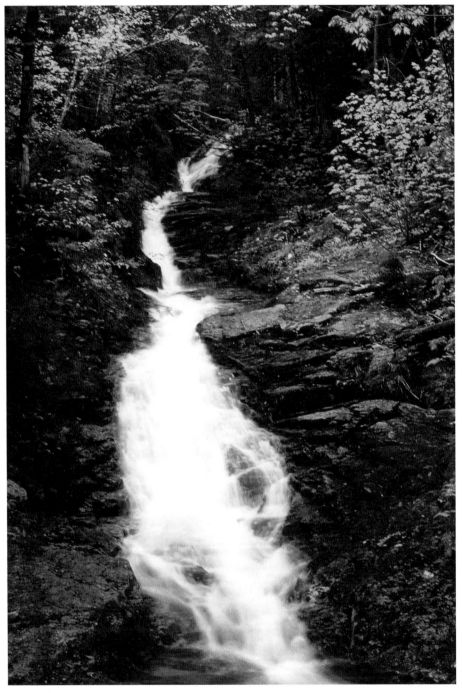

Kedron Flume

ROBERT J. KOZLOW

running trains through the notch. So the track is in use again, and you should be careful as you cross it to the trail's log-and-rock steps on the other side.

The trail continues steep. Although graded, with switchbacks, it is a mountain trail. The soft stone gravel will roll underfoot. Watch your step, especially descending. The trail leads through beech woods toward spruces farther on. It bends around a shoulder and dips into a little ravine at Kedron Brook.

The stream pours down through a narrow sluice or flume in the rock and drops over the falls below the trail's crossing. Remember that rocks are slippery when wet. The outlook across the notch's gash is to Mount Webster's southern ridge and minor cliffs.

For 0.5 mile past the flume, the trail twists more steeply up among big spruces and rocks to its junction with the Ethan Pond Trail, a route into the Pemigewasset Wilderness past the Willey Range Trail up Mount Willey, which towers above Kedron Flume.

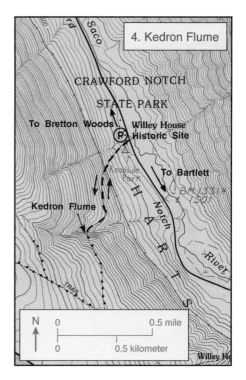

5

Three Ponds–Brown Brook Loop

Distance (round trip): 5½ miles
Walking time: 3½ hours
Vertical rise: 500 feet
Maps: USDA/FS 7½' Mt. Kineo; USGS 7½' Mt. Kineo

A hike to Three Ponds and across a height-of-land to another watershed on Brown Brook is a leg-stretcher and fine for gaining woods experience. A weekend in June is a good time to visit this forest environment of boggy ponds, beaver dams, hardwoods, and evergreens. Wildflowers, then abundant, will include pink lady's slipper, the little yellow flowers of clintonia, and carpets of Canada mayflower. White-throated sparrows give their haunting, North Country whistles. Joining in will be all the returned birds.

But take plenty of fly dope. Blackflies will welcome you in June. Tuck long pants into socks. A head net is a wise precaution.

Be prepared for trail changes caused by beaver activity and blowdowns.

HOW TO GET THERE

Drive along NH 25 west from Plymouth to the sign for Rumney Village. Turn north through Rumney, taking Main Street and Stinson Lake Road to Stinson Lake. Keep left on Stinson Lake Road along the west shore. The road changes to gravel. At 6.9 miles from NH 25, turn left at a hiker symbol, and park.

If you are coming from I-93, take Exit 28 in Campton and drive 9.3 miles on NH 49, Ellsworth Road, and Stinson Lake Road to the trailhead.

THE TRAIL

At the trailhead, a snowmobile trail marked with a red diamond departs to the left. Take the Three Ponds Trail, blazed yellow, which

5. Three Ponds–Brown Brook Loop

N   0   0.5 mile
     0   0.5 kilometer

Foxglove
Pond

2020×

Three Ponds
TRAIL

DONKEY HILL

CUTOFF

1725

Shelter

×2105

2000

Brown
MOUNT KINEO TRAIL

1600

Brook

Mount Kineo Tr

1400

405

1800

2000

2135 × Black Hill

Sucker

THREE   PONDS

bridge

Three Ponds Tr

1600

1600

1311×

410
P

MOUNTAIN

1800

TRAIL

Brook

2000

2400

×2474

2200

1400

1371

1600

1303

BM
1310

Stinson
Lake

leads into the woods across bog bridges over a trickle of water. The Three Ponds Trail continues uphill among maples and birches interspersed with hemlocks and pines. Near the middle of this hill the Mount Kineo Trail leaves on the right. You will return here at the conclusion of the hike.

The trail keeps irregularly along the west slope of Black Hill and takes you past the Carr Mountain Trail. About a mile farther you descend to a footbridge over Sucker Brook and join an old logging road, the former trail. Turn to the right on it. You'll use snowmobile bridges for the next crossings, make two bridgeless crossings, then negotiate the re-located trail before you find yourself on the trail again.

As you approach the ponds, Middle Pond appears on your left. Watch for a path on the right up a steep bank. It leads to the Three Ponds Shelter, on a knoll. South of it, hidden by trees and brush, lies the smallest pond, called Lower Pond. Hardly worth visiting, it covers just 2.5 acres compared to Middle Pond's 13 acres.

The trail continues through the woods bordering Middle Pond. Toward the end of the pond, take a path right to avoid a boggy area. Shortly thereafter you come to a trail junction. The Three Ponds Trail turns left. Straight ahead the Donkey Hill Cutoff will be your link to the Mount Kineo Trail and Brown Brook.

But before continuing on the Donkey Hill Cutoff, take a side trip to unique Third, or Upper, Pond. Turn left along the Three Ponds Trail. Previously, you could cross an abandoned beaver dam, which was easier said than done. In recent years, beavers have built a new dam and have flooded the area. If you are able to get across, you'll find that the trail becomes a logging road for about 0.25 mile to Upper Pond. A hundred yards before the pond, the Three Ponds Trail branches left.

On Three Ponds Trail   ROBERT J. KOZLOW

You continue straight to Upper Pond. (The Three Ponds Trail traverses forest to the Hubbard Brook Trail and NH 118, about 4 miles away.)

The 12 acres of water at its deepest is 10 feet, or 4 feet less than the 14 feet for Middle Pond, but it floods into coves and boggy growths of waterbrush and evergreens. A gentle slope of woods on the south grows luxuriant wildflowers around old campsites of trout fishermen. Perhaps there'll be a swimming black duck suddenly beating aloft from the water, possibly a mink or beaver if you wait silently on shore and listen to the thrushes. After a heavy rain, you hear the falls splashing down the west ridge into the pond from tiny Foxglove Pond.

Return to the junction with the Donkey Hill Cutoff. Turn left. The Donkey Hill Cutoff is rather obscure as it bears right past beaver flooding. Then it swings sharp left to take the route of an old logging road. Climbing slightly but steadily, you cross the imperceptible height-of-land and descend more abruptly toward the bogs and beaver flowages of Brown Brook. Avoiding this wet tangle, after a view toward Mount Kineo, the trail climbs a small ridge and turns sharply right, south. You follow up and down several ridges and valleys, then swing west around a spruce swamp to the junction with the Mount Kineo Trail. Here, at ledges over which

Brown Brook flows and tumbles down into lower hardwoods from the spruces, the Mount Kineo Trail crosses to the far bank. (The Mount Kineo Trail heads northward over a shoulder of Mount Kineo 3.5 miles to a forest service road in the Hubbard Brook Experimental Forest.)

Keep straight down Brown Brook on the Mount Kineo Trail. Had you been dropped blindfolded from a helicopter along it, you'd easily mistake the trail for the logging road you followed near Middle Pond. It keeps to the west bank of the brook for about 1 mile, then bears away to the right as a woods trail. Watch for yellow blazes on trees.

This section of the Mount Kineo Trail leaves the valley of Brown Brook, climbing slightly across a ridge to the junction with the Three Ponds Trail. Turn left for the short walk down to your car.

6

East Pond

Distance (Tripoli Road to East Pond and back): 3 miles

Walking time: 2½ hours

Vertical rise: 780 feet

Maps: USDA/FS 7½' Mt. Osceola; USGS 7½' Mt. Osceola; USDA/FS 7½' Waterville Valley; USGS 7½' Waterville Valley

In its simple wooded setting, with Scar Ridge and Mount Osceola's West Peak in the background, East Pond resembles many small, high lakes, which nestle among the ridges and mountains surrounding the more impressive and famous peaks. Yet each is individual, a special goal for a hike. East Pond covers 6.5 acres. Much of the shore is lined with rocks or gravel and sand. The water is cool and clear; it reaches depths of as much as 27 feet and provides shelter for speckled trout, which seem inclined to stay there.

Across Scar Ridge's spruce-grown slopes, green lines indicate the routes of old logging roads. Scrap iron and bolts lie in the sand near the pond's outlet, relics of dredging for diatomaceous earth years ago. A ditch guides the little brook to its drop-off into the valley. In late September, berries of several mountain ash trees cluster in scarlet splashes above the shore and against the ridge, making a Christmas-like display of green and red. In spring, snow lingers in protected hollows. Memorial Day hikers may still find a melting drift near the outlet.

HOW TO GET THERE

The shortest route to East Pond is from the Tripoli Road, which leads east off I-93 at Exit 31. It connects with the upper end of Waterville Valley and NH 49.

About 5 miles from Exit 31, watch on the left for the forest service signpost marking the start of the East Pond Trail. Turn left and drive up to a parking area.

Diatomaceous earth is also called tripolite; thus, Tripoli Road.

THE TRAIL

The trail begins as a gravel road to a clearing 0.5 mile up the ridge. When the road bears right into that opening, keep straight on the old trail. After a few yards you come to the Little East Pond Trail on the left (see note about East Pond Loop at end of the hike description), and you cross the railroad grade that once supported rails and trains servicing the Tripoli Mill to your right. Foundations still exist in the woods that grow from the site where the diatomaceous earth was processed.

Continue straight ahead as the trail rises gradually through hardwoods. You cross East Pond Brook, and begin to climb more steeply for the remaining 0.5 mile into evergreens until the trail levels out at the pond. Its elevation is 2,600 feet. To the left is the East Pond Loop. To the right, a short spur trail leads to East Pond's south shore.

For hikers climbing over Scar Ridge to the Kancamagus Highway, the East Pond Trail passes the south end of the pond and runs partway along the west shore before it swings away steeply and heads northeast for the height-of-land about 500 feet above the pond. Of course, a hiker crossing the 5 miles between the Tripoli Road and the Kancamagus must make arrangements for transportation at the end of the hike.

Note about East Pond Loop: This loop gives you the opportunity to see Little East Pond. It will take an additional hour of hiking and about 2 more miles than if you just hike to East Pond and back on the East Pond Trail. The loop's total length from the East Pond Trail trailhead is 5 miles.

At the south end of East Pond, where the East Pond Trail continues up the west side, the East Pond Loop branches left, west, nearly on the contour for 1.5 miles, going uphill and down in a leisurely fashion on the way to shallow Little East Pond. In contrast to East Pond's depth, here lily pads float on the surface above stems and roots long enough to feed on the bottom. The pads sometimes raise half their discs in response to the downdraft winds from Scar Ridge.

Leaving Little East Pond, the Little East Pond Trail follows the outlet at first. When it joins the old railroad grade, look for old rails along the trail. You cross Clear Brook in a ravine that makes you imagine a trestle. There are a noticeable number of white ash trees amid the other hardwoods in the stretch to the East Pond Brook crossing. After 1.7 miles, you reach the junction with the East Pond Trail. Here you turn right for the brief descent to your car.

Little East Pond doesn't provide a good picnic spot, so if the timing would suit you better, hike the loop in reverse, from Little East Pond to East Pond, where you can eat your lunch on the shore.

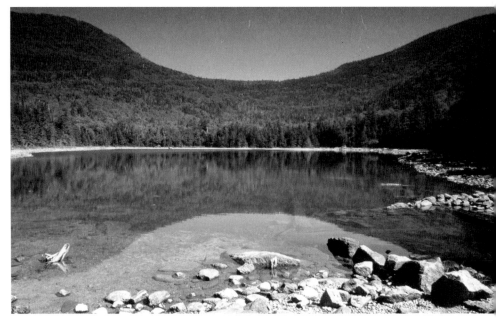

East Pond

Introductory Hikes

7

Greeley Ponds

Distance (round trip): 4 miles

Walking time: 2½ hours

Vertical rise: 400 feet

*Maps: USDA/FS 7½' Mt. Osceola;
USGS 7½' Mt. Osceola*

The west shoulder of Mount Kancamagus and Mount Osceola's precipitous East Peak frame the two Greeley Ponds in a wild and mountainous setting. The northern or upper pond below Mad River Notch reflects the western cliffs; the lower pond narrows between boggy shores grown to spruce and fir.

As an official National Forest Scenic Area, 810 acres surrounding Greeley Ponds are preserved in their natural beauty. To this end, the forest service has taken down the old log shelter by the upper pond, because, paradoxically, it was too popular. Sanitation problems, fuel requirements for the fireplace, garbage and rubbish disposal, and campsites extemporized nearby all despoiled the scanty earth, the pure water, and the slow-growing trees. People were overwhelming the delicate environment they had come to enjoy. So the forest service has asked overnighters to plan their trips elsewhere. Visit, but don't camp.

HOW TO GET THERE
Take Exit 32 off I-93, and drive through Lincoln onto the Kancamagus Highway past Otter Rocks Rest Area and the forest service's trail sign for East Pond on your right. Continue on to a sign on your right for the Greeley Ponds Trail parking. The distance from the exit to the parking area is 10.3 miles.

THE TRAIL
Beyond a small knoll, the yellow-blazed trail leads over bog bridges across wet seepages, with the walking often rough. The

7. Greeley Ponds

Kancamagus Hwy
To Conway →
To Lincoln →
Trail Parking
1940
Mad River Notch
GREELEY
2245
Greeley Ponds
PONDS
SCENIC
East Peak
AREA
Mad

0   0.25 mile
0   0.25 kilometer

the right. Beyond this, avoid the cross-country ski trail marked in blue. Your trail drops a short distance to the upper pond and follows under the cliffs along the west shore in evergreens. Near the outlet, a spur trail, left, leads around the end of the pond to the former shelter site.

Straight ahead, the Greeley Ponds Trail continues past a spring on the right a few yards and begins intersecting the ski trail, which in summer is usually wet and muddy. After 0.5 mile you come to the lower pond. Unlike the upper pond, it is narrow and shallow. (The Greeley Ponds Trail follows the valley southwest 3 miles through woods of conifers and deciduous trees along the young Mad River to so-called Depot Camp in Waterville Valley, now a clearing at the beginning of the Livermore Road.)

The upper pond has an area of 1.25 acres and a maximum depth of 27 feet. The lower pond averages 3 feet deep over its 2 acres. Beavers seem at home in both ponds. As a beaver swims past, his brown head leaves a wake like a toy powerboat. Alarmed, he whacks his tail on the water and dives immediately.

You may want to walk back to the upper pond to eat your sandwiches on the little beach. Spruces and pointed firs rise toward the cliff and reflect in the still water. Speckled trout break the surface to suck down hatching flies. Juncos and white-throated sparrows call from the trees. Cedar waxwings flutter over the pond to catch bugs, then return to a tree branch alongshore and preen their glossy feathers. Swallows skim above the spruces or dip into the pond for an instant of a skimming arc after insects. Dragonflies patrol the airways.

From the towering western cliff I once saw a peregrine falcon dive like a winged projectile at a black duck on the pond. The duck submerged at the last moment and escaped.

bridge over the South Fork of Hancock Branch has been removed. Turn right after this crossing, following the blazes.

Then you climb easily to Mad River Notch, where the Mount Osceola Trail diverges on

Upper Greeley Pond

The peregrine spread his wings and shot upward into hunting circles before giving up and flying off toward the lower pond area. The duck finally appeared cautiously in the brush along the west shore. This was in 1947 before the disastrous effects of DDT almost exterminated peregrines, ospreys, and eagles. Now these raptors are recovering.

After you linger close to this intrinsically wild harmony of water, rocks, and trees, return to your car by the same route you came up.

A NOTE ON OVERUSE

The popularity of the mountains creates a problem for the forest service, the Appalachian Mountain Club and other mountain clubs, and, in fact, all conservationists and all citizens: overuse.

Hikers, like all humankind, congregate, and so destroy the primitive environment they seek. On Mount Washington, Tucker-man Ravine camping had to be restricted to protect the trees, plants, and soil; they are responding. In the Franconia Range, the Liberty Spring Shelter has been replaced by tent platforms. Campfire and camping regulations throughout the White Mountain National Forest have been extended to preserve the forests and the areas above treeline. The problem became so serious that the forest service established Forest Protection Areas to allow natural recovery of damaged land, trees, plants, and water. Soil erosion, vegetation loss, water pollution, and compaction of soil, usually at campsites, are examples of environmental damage that hikers can cause. Excessive use of campfires and the accompanying destruction of the wood resource are also in need of control. Obviously, dispersal of hikers is necessary, and an important aim of the program.

Easy access to the mountains is certainly not the whole problem, but it may be part of it. The Kancamagus Highway accounts in some measure for the popularity of Greeley Ponds and the consequent overuse, classification as a Forest Protection Area, and removal of the shelter. (Some recalcitrant old-timers think the cross-mountain road between Lincoln and Conway never should have been built.)

The Greeley Ponds area is recovering, and I like to think that hikers are learning to be more careful of the forest and mountains. I am encouraged by the improvement in the litter situation along trails and at campsites. Hikers are responding to the motto "Carry in, carry out." They are also taking to heart more and more (I believe and hope) the ethics of good camping and hiking practices. You can do the same by following the restrictions in the forest service's "Backcountry Camping Rules." (See Introduction.)

With care and preservation, the mountains can be a continuing source of "wildness" in the deepest sense, of life force from the trees, moss, lichens, birds, and animals—but only if humans control their own "wildness."

8

Old Mast Road and Kelley Trail

Distance (round trip): 5 miles
Walking time: 3¼ hours
Vertical rise: 1,000 feet
Maps: USDA/FS 7½' Mt. Chocorua; USGS 15' Mt. Chocorua

The loop from Wonalancet over the Old Mast Road and the Kelley Trail connects with other trails between NH 113A and the Kancamagus Highway. The area offers hikes and climbs of varied distances and destinations in the Sandwich Range—mountains that extend west from Mount Chocorua and include Mount Paugus, Mount Passaconaway, Sandwich Mountain, and others north of the Lakes Region.

A hike need not be a physical challenge. Woods walking provides the satisfactions of escape and seclusion, as well as the pleasures of striding and breathing deeply. For these purposes, the Old Mast Road–Kelley Trail combination is ideal.

According to legend, the Old Mast Road was first cut through the primeval forest to haul out great masts for the British navy. The trail's ascent up even contours toward Paugus Pass, and the long stretches without a turn, would seem to bear out the legend. For contrast, the return route takes you scrambling down Cold Brook via the Kelley Trail. (If you are hiking with young children, it would perhaps be better to do the hike in reverse so that their energy will be high for the rocks of the Cold Brook ravine.)

The Wonalancet Out Door Club's colorful map is very useful. See www.wodc.org.

HOW TO GET THERE

Drive to Wonalancet on NH 113A from North Sandwich or Tamworth. Near the picturesque Wonalancet Union Chapel, turn off NH 113A onto Ferncroft Road. Drive a scant 0.5 mile to a road on the right. You'll see a hiker sign. Turn in to the Ferncroft kiosk and parking.

THE TRAIL

Walk along the road from the parking area to the woods. At a fork and gates, turn left onto the Old Mast Road and the Kelley Trail.

You soon come to a bridge over a brook. (The Wonalancet Range Trail starts up on your left for those wooded summits and the Walden Trail.) At 0.3 mile the Kelley Trail branches off to the right. This will be your return route.

The Old Mast Road becomes an unused logging road up a steady grade. You climb through a forest of beech and yellow birch. The rugged, older yellow birches have a reddish-brown-gray bark, scaly and furrowed, as though a different species from the younger trees with their pale yellow bark that peels across the trunks in ribbons and layers. Their leaves resemble those of the white birches sometimes growing nearby.

Easily distinguished are the smooth, gray beech trunks common along the trail, which they shade by extending their muscular branches almost horizontally. The branches end in slender twigs and light green leaves; the delicacy seems to belie their strength. The burrs enclosing the triangular nuts begin to open in late August, to the delight of squirrels and blue jays. Bears also feast on the beechnuts by climbing into the branches. Keep looking at the gray trunks, and you'll see the healed gouges of claw marks—but probably no fresh ones.

During a warm, damp August, many mushroom varieties appear almost overnight. There are edible and inedible varieties, and, of course, some very poisonous ones. Among the toxic varieties are the deadly amanita, both the yellow type and the white species known as the Destroying Angel. Fragrant orange chanterelle, smelling of apricots

8. Old Mast Road and Kelley Trail

Introductory Hikes

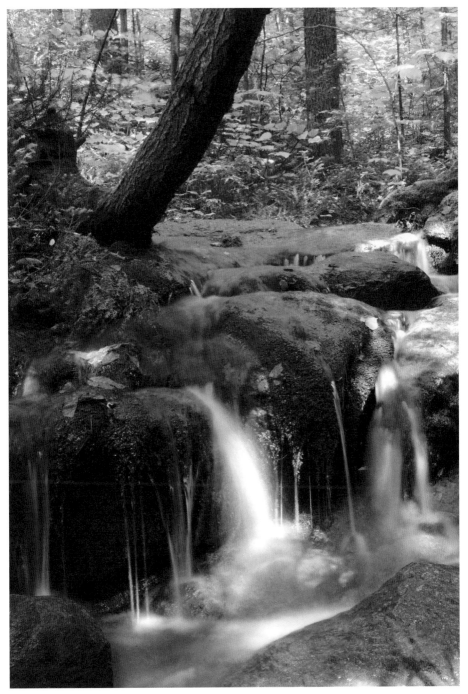

On Kelley Trail

ROBERT J. KOZLOW

when warmed in your hand, shaped like a little inverted twisted saucer on a stem, is a gourmet's delight. But, unless you are an expert on the various species, don't take chances by eating any of them.

Birds along the trail, such as thrushes, are typical of the deep woods, although a scarlet tanager sometimes flits and calls among the high branches, or a fluttering redstart flashes among smaller trees.

After 2.5 miles, the Old Mast Road terminates at a junction on the height-of-land named Paugus Pass. Continuing north, descending, rough, is the Square Ledge Trail. Left, or west, the Walden Trail leads up Mount Passaconaway. Right, or east, the Lawrence Trail crosses the pass and climbs Mount Paugus. The Lawrence Trail also leads to the Kelley Trail. You are briefly in the Sandwich Range Wilderness.

Turn right, east, on the Lawrence Trail, and follow it 0.5 mile to the Kelley Trail. At their junction, the Lawrence Trail continues its rough and steep ascent east up Mount Paugus. To the left (north) the Oliverian Brook Trail leads, after about 4.5 miles through wet ground along Oliverian Brook,

to the Kancamagus Highway. For your return to Wonalancet, turn right, south, and follow the Kelley Trail into the ravine of Cold Brook.

Here you must concentrate on your footing. The trail descends over bedrock and past glacial falls and through gloomy, cool woods of big spruces. A ledge split again and again looks like the stonework of an expert mason. There may be deer tracks on the miniature sandbars, maybe a winter wren on a mossy log, trilling like a coloratura canary. Lush woodland ferns grow from dark humus and curve over rocks. Hobblebush blossoms are white in early summer—they turn to green berries later, then red. Graceful gray-green lichens thrive on ledges.

The trail crosses the brook, recrosses, and crosses again. After a little waterfall, it veers away from the brook. As you approach the last section of the trail, you come to a logging road. Turn right and walk up the road about 100 yards to a Kelley Trail sign and blue blaze on the left. The trail enters the woods and in 0.25 mile joins the Old Mast Road. Turn left and follow the Old Mast Road back to the parking area.

Belknap Mountain

Distance (round trip): 2 miles

Walking time: 2 hours

Vertical rise: 740 feet

Maps: USGS 7½' Laconia; USGS 7½' West Alton

A short climb to the lookout tower atop Belknap Mountain opens a view across Lake Winnipesaukee's blue water and many islands. The Ossipee Mountains rise beyond in impressive array, green ridge upon green ridge forming a long single mountain from this distance. To the left, 50 miles away and unmistakable in spring and fall when it alone displays snow, Mount Washington appears distant yet splendid. Nearer and somewhat in line, peaks of the central and west Sandwich Range group themselves beyond the far end of Lake Winnipesaukee. Still more to the left and again distant, the line of rocky Franconia Range is dominated by Mount Lafayette. Foothills around Mount Moosilauke fill in the panorama continuing west. On a sunny day the passing high clouds shift light and shadows upon the lake and mountains.

Of the four summits in this small, circular range south of Lake Winnipesaukee, Belknap Mountain is the highest, although perhaps not so well known as Gunstock Mountain, with its ski area of the same name. Gunstock Mountain and Mount Rowe are usually climbed by trails from this ski area. The fourth summit, Piper Mountain, is a bare ridge to the south. Belknap Mountain offers not only the highest summit, 2,382 feet, but also a mountain drive to a picnic area.

HOW TO GET THERE

Turn off NH 11A at Gilford onto the Belknap Mountain Road, and proceed south through the village. At 0.8 mile the road makes a left turn and climbs to the top of a ridge; then at

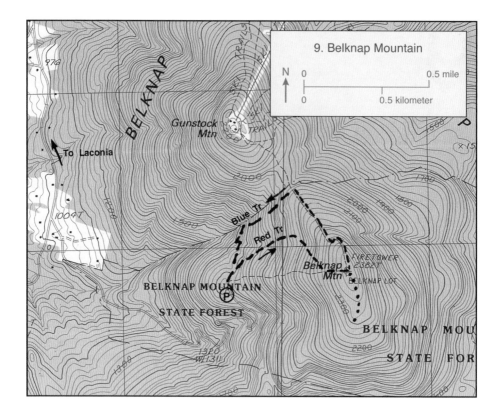

9. Belknap Mountain

1.3 miles it turns sharply right and continues south under the mountain slopes. At 2.4 miles from NH 11A, take a left onto the Carriage Road at a Belknap Mountain sign. Another sign warns you that the gate ahead is closed from 6 PM to 9 AM. The Carriage Road leads into a steep valley, winds upward, changes to gravel, resorts to switchbacks, and ends in 1.5 miles at a level parking area.

THE TRAIL

For the trails to the summit, walk uphill along the continuation of the road and past a small garage. The Red Trail begins on the right a few yards along a woods road. The path enters the woods and is identified by red paint blazes. It rises steadily and becomes more of a mountain trail as it bears right into spruces and passes an outlook to the west with a view of Kearsarge in the distance. Continue climbing uphill. Through the spruces you see sheds. The summit is directly beyond, surrounded by spruces; ledges support the steel fire tower.

Belknap Mountain is worth climbing even on a hazy day. Although distant mountains are obscured, the nearer Lakes Region and Lake Winnipesaukee's varied shorelines appear in a bird's-eye view. The lake is busy with boats. There is activity and traffic on roads in the Laconia–Weirs Beach area. For contrast, the woods stretch away east to the bare summit of Mount Major. Belknap Mountain's blueberries resemble packaged varieties in supermarkets, but a handful will remind you what blueberries are supposed to taste like.

Do not descend the Green Trail, which has become eroded. Take the Blue Trail down through a good mixture of conifers and hardwoods, and watch for signs of bear, moose, deer, and turkeys.

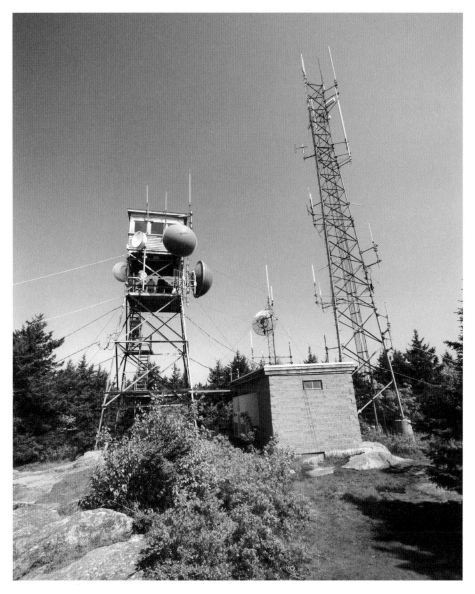

Belknap Mountain towers

10

Mount Katherine

Distance: 3¼ miles	
Walking time: 2½ hours	
Vertical rise: 250 feet	
Maps: USGS 7½' Mt. Chocorua	

From the ledges on Mount Katherine's 1,380-foot summit, you look across at Mount Chocorua and down on the beautiful Birch Intervale (Wonalancet Intervale) that you drove through to reach the trailhead. The trees that surround the ledges grow a little taller every year, but these views are still a satisfying reward for a simple hike.

Mount Katherine is named for Katherine Sleeper Walden, who was instrumental in the creation of trails in the Wonalancet area. The granddaughter of the editor of a Boston newspaper, Kate became a reporter in Boston before she visited Tamworth in 1890 and decided to stay. She bought a farm, named it Wonalancet Farm, and with her husband ran it as an inn, into the 1930s. In 1898 she organized the Wonalancet Out Door Club.

Her husband, Arthur Walden, trained sled dogs, including the famous Chinook and other dogs that Admiral Richard Byrd used on his first expedition to the Antarctic.

As with the Old Mast Road and Kelley Trail (Hike 8), the Wonalancet Out Door Club's map is handy to have. See www .wodc.org.

HOW TO GET THERE

Drive to Wonalancet on NH 113A from North Sandwich or Tamworth. Near the Wonalancet Union Chapel, turn off NH 113A onto Ferncroft Road. Drive 0.5 mile to a road on the right. There is a hiker sign. Turn in to the Ferncroft kiosk and parking.

The long-gone Ferncroft Inn gave its name to this vicinity.

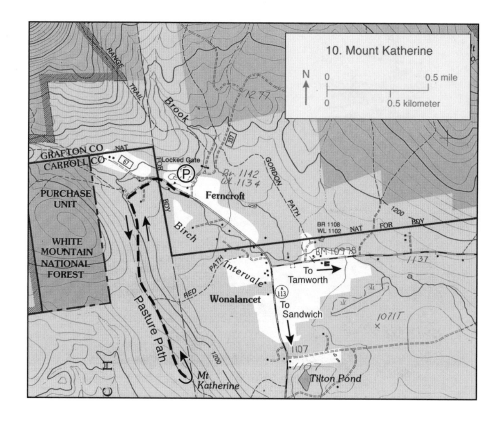

THE TRAIL

When you leave the parking area, turn right. For 0.3 mile the Blueberry Ledge Trail is the Ferncroft Road, leading you to Squirrel Bridge on your left and across the bridge. Bear right at a trail sign, away from a private driveway, and continue following the Blueberry Ledge Trail until the Pasture Path begins on the left. The Blueberry Ledge Trail turns right and eventually ascends Mount Whiteface.

Take the Pasture Path. It's a trail of moss and ferns and dappled, flickering light. As you walk up the pleasant incline you'll see stone walls that prove that where these trees now grow there once was pasture.

After you progress uphill, downhill, uphill, at 0.6 mile you come to Tilton Spring. Its water is piped into a stone-lined pool, with a busy yet peaceful sound. This is a junction where the Red Path goes left and the Tilton Spring Path goes right. You continue straight ahead on the Pasture Path, which proceeds for 0.5 mile on its easy way up past a view of Mount Whiteface and reaches Mount Katherine's summit ledges, where those views of Chocorua and the Intervale, as well as the Sandwich Range, await you.

Return down the Pasture Path to Tilton Spring. Here you have choices. You can take the Red Path for a quicker descent but then

View from Mount Katherine   RUTH DOAN MACDOUGALL

a longer walk on the road back to the parking area. If you do this loop, your total mileage for the hike is 3.4 miles, with a 300-foot vertical rise. Or you can make a loop via the Tilton Spring Path and the McCrillis Path back to the Blueberry Ledge Trail for a total of 4.1 miles, with a 450-foot vertical rise. Or you can continue down the Pasture Path to the Blueberry Ledge Trail, Squirrel Bridge, and Ferncroft Road.

Introductory Hikes

11

Mount Major

Distance (round trip): 3 miles
Walking time: 2½ hours
Vertical rise: 1,150 feet
Map: USGS 7½' West Alton

Steep, wooded slopes and ledges hide this bare summit (1,786 feet) above Lake Winnipesaukee's Alton Bay. Mount Major surprises you with the extent of the outlook in all directions, but you are primarily attracted to the lake, for this is a lakeshore mountain.

Another surprise is the difficulty of the ledges. Be careful in wet or icy weather, or choose another hike.

HOW TO GET THERE

From the junction of NH 11 and NH 11B in Gilford, drive NH 11 southeast along Lake Winnipesaukee for 9 miles. A highway sign identifies the parking area for the Mount Major Trail. If you are coming northwest from Alton Bay on NH 11, you'll reach the parking area in 4.2 miles.

THE TRAIL

The trail, actually a logging road, enters a little valley of oaks, maples, and hemlocks. Almost at once it forks. Keep right. Two informal branches to the left rejoin the main trail at the top of the steady rise.

Soon you follow a westering curve at the junction with the left fork. The road levels along the north shoulder of the mountain. Check your watch because your turn upward toward the summit is only 10 minutes away. Old stone walls parallel the road or strike off among the oaks.

At about 0.7 mile, watch for blue-blazed arrows pointing left. Turn off the logging road, and continue your climb on the true mountain footpath. It winds over rocks and among pines. It grows steeper and

11. Mount Major

N

0   0.5 mile

0   0.5 kilometer

To Laconia

Mt Major

925 AT

1077 AT

Woodmans Cove

BM 518.1
S. END OF CLEARING S\S

1-163
616 T

Mt Major Tr

Mt Major

Mt MAJOR
STATE PARK

Brookhurst

639 T

Lake Winnipesaukee

WASHINGTON

MT

BM 524.9
RD ⓔ DR 526

To Alton   Pumpki
Point

Cedar
Mtn

approaches the first ledges. In early June, there are pink lady's slippers flowering. Columbine blossoms beside the rocks. At the ledges, pause to look behind you for the first high views of Lake Winnipesaukee.

Low-bush blueberries grow along the trail. Wild cherries, pines, young white birch, and mountain maple extend into the blueberry patches. The trail reaches the final ledges, which may look daunting to you. You'll see a sign that says you can choose to take the "Main Trail ledge detour." If you choose the "Main Trail via ledges," use cau-

tion. These ledges are at first sharp and in places sheer for a few feet, putting you to handholds and careful footholds. This is scrambling, not rock climbing. The upper ledges are worn away by glaciers and by exposure, but the coarse, notched surfaces are readily surmounted.

On the open summit, a four-sided roofless stone shelter stands out against the sky. Its rock slabs are mortared into walls. It was built in 1925 by George M. Phippen, a lifelong summer resident of Alton Bay. Winter winds took off two roofs. From this landmark

     Introductory Hikes

various outlooks open in all directions. The views sweep around you, but the lake catches and holds your attention.

Long and narrow, Alton Bay extends to the south. Northward the big lake stretches to the east shore and the town of Wolfeboro. Directly north is the length of Rattlesnake Island. Beyond, the blue water extends northwesterly, broken by many islands and peninsulas, or "necks," which blend in the distance with the reaches of the lake and wooded slopes rising to the Sandwich Range and Ossipee Mountains. Often in summer, haze obscures the farther peaks, but on a day of real clarity you can see Mount Moosilauke, the tips of one or two Franconias, Sandwich Mountain, Whiteface, Passaconaway, and rising behind Ossipee's long ridge—Mount Washington. To the west, Belknap Mountain's tower marks that summit, above lesser, forested ridges.

Mount Major, open rock except for blueberry bushes and small birches, exposes you to cooling breezes, welcome after the climb.

Descend by the same route. For variety or in bad weather, take the blue-blazed route toward Straightback Mountain and continue down by the yellow-blazed Brook Trail 1.7 miles to rejoin the Mount Major Trail. From here it's 0.7 mile back to the parking area.

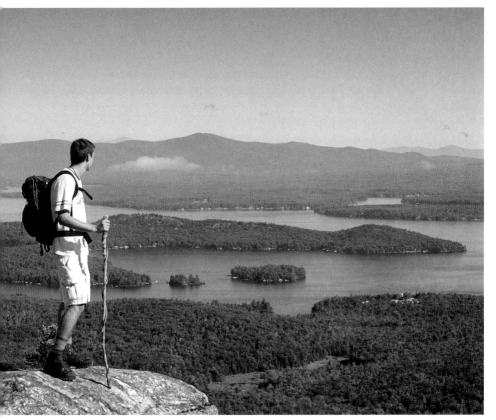

Lake Winnipesaukee from Mount Major   ROBERT J. KOZLOW

12

Hedgehog Mountain

Distance (round trip): 5 miles

Walking time: 3½ hours

Vertical rise: 1,350 feet

Maps: USDA/FS 7½' Mount Chocorua; USGS 7½' Mount Chocorua

Rising between the valleys of Oliverian Brook on the east and Downes Brook on the west, Hedgehog Mountain, at 2,532 feet, contains a variety of pleasures: a simple loop trail, woodsy walking, scrambling up ledges, and views both wide and fringed.

HOW TO GET THERE

From the east, turn off NH 16 in Conway onto the Kancamagus Highway (NH 112), and drive about 14.3 miles. From the west on I-93, take Exit 32 in Lincoln, and drive about 21.8 miles on the Kancamagus.

You'll see a sign for the turn to the trailheads on the south side of the highway: the Downes Brook, UNH, and Mount Potash Trails. Turn here and drive in to the large parking area.

THE TRAIL

A University of New Hampshire forestry camp in the area gave the UNH Trail its name. It swings left off the Downes Brook Trail after 60 yards. Follow the UNH Trail. Here an old railroad grade, it has the broad stateliness of a promenade and gives you a brief warm-up for the hike, the forest glowing green and golden in the morning sun.

At 0.2 mile, the hike used to start up the eastern side of the loop, but this part of the trail has now been bypassed because of erosion. A sign directs you to the right, up the western side of the loop. At 0.8 mile a new section of the trail turns to the left across the slope and joins the old eastern route in 0.3 mile, turning right. You are now traveling clockwise, for the best viewing. The trail crosses White Brook. On you climb, up over roots and rocks, and soon the trail begins to become exposed over ledges.

Then, at 2 miles, the east ledges spread out before you, with their views south and southeast. Be wary of some sheer drop-offs as you gaze at Mount Passaconaway, Mount Paugus, Mount Chocorua, and the Moats.

Continuing onward, you see the summit of Hedgehog ahead. Make sure you keep looking for the yellow blazes on the ledges; some are faded, and it is easy to lose the trail.

After you reenter the woods, the trail twists up and down until you are circling up under the boulders of the summit. Reaching the top at 2.9 miles, you have a closer view of the mountains you saw at the east ledges, as well as the eastern slope of Mount Tripyramid. From another ledge, to the left of the summit, you'll find wider views to the north, west, and south. So you have a choice of ledges and views for a lunch spot.

When you leave the summit, follow the yellow blazes. Views to the north and west open up through the trees, and if the weather is clear enough you can even see Mount Washington. You can also see the Presiden-

On Hedgehog Mountain   ROBERT J. KOZLOW

tial Range, the Carrigain Range, North and South Twins, Franconia Ridge, Mount Willey, and the Bonds.

This view is the feature of Allen's Ledge, which you come to at 3.7 miles, where a steep side trail to the right leads you 60 yards to the two-level lookoff. And here again are Paugus and Chocorua. The ledge is named after Jack Allen, an early White Mountains guide.

Return to the main trail and continue down to the loop junction and that grand promenade of the morning.

13

Stinson Mountain

Distance (round trip): 3½ miles

Walking time: 2 hours

Vertical rise: 1,400 feet

Maps: USDA/FS 7½' Rumney; USGS 7½' Rumney

Alone and easily accessible from the Baker River valley, Stinson Mountain has the specialties and charms of smaller mountains. Its elevation of 2,900 feet treats the hiker to the joy of arriving at the summit after just enough effort and distance to impart a sense of accomplishment. This delight, compounded of well-being, good luck, and the wide view, has more to do with why people climb mountains than the commonly accepted motive "because it's there."

The summit ledges, once the site of a fire tower, offer fine views, although the vistas to the north are now partially obscured by trees. Forests, mountains, and lakes surround the lovely rural valley along Baker River, with its farms and houses. The Franconia Range and the Sandwich Range are north and east. The village of Rumney lies at the foot of the mountain, Stinson Lake in the hollow to the north, Campton Bog to the east. Lesser-known mountains on the west—Mount Cube, Smarts Mountain, Piermont Mountain, Carr Mountain—are clothed in forests. To the north, Mount Moosilauke rises above treeline.

Pleasant and varied in any season from spring to late fall, Stinson Mountain is especially fine in October, not only for the trail, which rises through leafed woods of red and yellow, but also for the blends of colors spreading out in all directions from the summit. By then the cone of Mount Moosilauke is sometimes snowcapped.

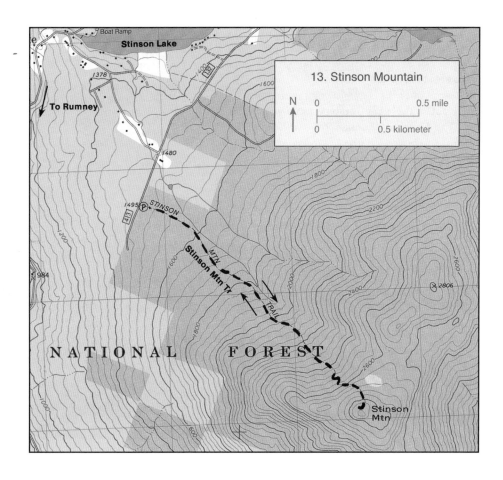

HOW TO GET THERE

Drive west from Plymouth on NH 25 to the sign for Rumney Village. Turn north through the village, taking Main Street and Stinson Lake Road 5.1 miles to Stinson Lake. Bear right near the outlet of the lake onto Cross Road, and continue uphill 0.8 mile. Swing to the right onto a road less traveled, Lower Doe Town Road, and drive 0.3 mile to parking on the left at the start of the trail.

THE TRAIL

The Stinson Mountain Trail leads into open woods and along stone walls to an old cellar hole, which it passes on a left corner. Large trees grow from the cellar, demonstrating the many years since (probably) the roof of the farmhouse fell in after the family moved west or became city folks.

The trail ascends gradually to a trickling brook. Here you begin the real climb by turning right and going up the steep slope. The trail alternately switches from steep grades to easier old logging roads. At about 1 mile, in the spring or fall you'll have a view of Stinson Lake; in summer, leaves hide it. Next, you come to a junction where a snowmobile trail on an old logging road branches left. Follow the Stinson Mountain Trail, right. Again you can glimpse Stinson Lake along here if the trees aren't leafed out.

As you near the summit, you meet the snowmobile trail again, coming in on your left. The Stinson Mountain Trail, straight ahead, enters spruce and fir woods interspersed with striped maple and mountain ash for the last climb and breaks out all at once into the clearing at the ledges.

But if you'd prefer to see the western view first, at the junction below the summit take the trail to the right and then follow a spur trail to see Stinson Lake, Carr Mountain, Mount Kineo, and Mount Moosilauke. Return to the trail, and continue up the ledges to the summit.

Here, you can enjoy your lunch (the footings for the old tower provide luxurious seating) and the panorama. Starting at the southeast, you are looking at Lake Winnipesaukee, Squam Lake, the Belknaps, Ragged Mountain, Mount Cardigan, and Mount Sunapee. In the foreground are Hersey Mountain, Plymouth Mountain, Newfound Lake, and Tenney Mountain.

Descend the way you came up, being careful at junctions.

View from Stinson Mountain   ROBERT J. KOZLOW

14

Mount Cardigan

Distance (around the loop): 3½ miles

Walking time: 2½ hours

Vertical rise: 1,300 feet

Maps: USGS 7½' Mt. Cardigan; USGS 15' Cardigan

A crown of solid rock forms the top of Mount Cardigan. As you approach the fire tower lookout exposed to the open sky and wind, you are taken by the illusion of climbing on the barren rock of some remote and mightier mountain; instead, you are on an outpost of the White Mountains at only 3,155 feet elevation. The illusion is dispelled by the sight of initials and dates carved in the rock over the years. Cardigan has been a popular climb for a long time, and many trails ascend it.

The route of this hike is a loop from Mount Cardigan State Park's parking and picnic area up the West Ridge Trail and back via South Peak and the South Ridge Trail. Access roads approach through the towns west of the mountain, Canaan and Orange.

Cardigan's distinctive rock dome is extended by the lower ledges of the north and south ridges. The rock is known as Cardigan pluton. It is a form of Kinsman quartz monzonite common in New Hampshire and is part of a formation at various levels, 60 miles long and 12 miles wide, extending from West Peterborough to north of Groton.

Here on Cardigan, forest fires destroyed the trees and organic earth, and erosion exposed the bare rock. In 1855, a fire twisted up in flame and smoke from the north ridge so spectacularly, and with such destruction, that the rock is still largely barren. The ridge is named "Firescrew," for the spiraling smoke and flames that were visible in all the villages for miles around.

The south ridge is also open rock, with only scattered evergreens. Views from South

14. Mount Cardigan

Peak are mostly east and west. But pick a clear day. Summer haze, which spoils the view, can sometimes be avoided by making an early morning climb.

About the first week in May, the lower forested slopes of hardwoods show the greenery of new leaves while trees above are still bare or only budded. In the fall, the first yellow and red leaves appear near the summit, while the lower trees remain green. Changes requiring weeks at a single elevation appear in one glance down the mountainside.

In spring and fall, watch out for ice on the rock. You could slide a long way into the trees with time to think about other errors before the crash.

Growing below the South Peak's ridge in May are dogtooth violets—really members of the lily family—and small yellow violets, purple trillium, and wood anemone. In summer, look for the flat leaves of the green-flowered orchis.

Binoculars are useful to study the lakes and farther ranges, or to peer into towns, or to watch a raven near the summit. This bird from the north has been seen on Cardigan. Warblers flock to the wooded slopes at migration time.

The summit receives the full blast of the wind. If the fire warden is in on a windy day, a climb to the lookout gives you an unbelievable "ride." The glassed-in room seems to rush downward with a rocking, roaring rumble, straining against the cables. In a high wind, the room sounds and feels like a subway car.

The view, starting west and looking counterclockwise, extends to Vermont, then Massachusetts, then east over the New Hampshire Lakes Region and the Belknaps, and around to the northeast, where the Sandwich Range is moored by the pinnacle of Mount Chocorua. Perhaps the clouds swirl over the distant Presidentials and Franconias. Mount Moosilauke, northward, may be impressively white in early spring and late fall. To the northwest, where four townships meet by Bryant Pond, a ridge running south is scarred by old mica mines.

HOW TO GET THERE

To reach the west side of the mountain and the West Ridge Trail, drive to Canaan on US 4. Turn north on NH 118, and soon take a right at a sign for Mt. Cardigan State Park. Drive into Orange, following the Cardigan signs 4.1 miles to the parking area and picnic tables.

THE TRAIL

The West Ridge Trail leaves the picnic clearing at a sign on the edge of the woods and climbs by easy stages. Keep left past the South Ridge Trail, which offers the best views as part of the return loop. Look ahead frequently for the West Ridge Trail's orange blazes; keep an especially sharp eye out

View from Mount Cardigan

when you approach one of the numerous branching paths that are not your route.

Walk past the Skyland Trail, which is a ridge route to Alexandria Four Corners. At about 1 mile, the West Ridge Trail crosses a footbridge named Cliff's Bridge. It then leads past the site of the old shelter, passes a branch trail, and ascends steeply over rock, along a route identified by cairns and orange paint, to the lookout tower.

In descending, follow the white blazes on the rock down to the fire lookout's cabin, bear right from the junction with the Clark Trail, and take the South Ridge Trail, blazed white. At the next trail signs, turn left for South Peak and Rimrock. The trail leads you over partially wooded ledges beyond South Peak, with its great views, to Rimrock and then crosses the Skyland Trail. The blazes for the South Ridge Trail now become orange. It descends steeply and slabs around through woods to the West Ridge Trail at the junction you passed on the way up, 0.5 mile above the parking area.

15

Smarts Mountain

Distance (round trip): 6½ miles
Walking time: 4½ hours
Vertical rise: 1,900 feet
Map: USGS 7½' Smarts Mountain

Although only 3,238 feet in elevation, Smarts Mountain provides excellent views from its now disused steel fire tower. You look up and down the Connecticut River Valley and over into Vermont. Northern mountains extend all the way to the Presidential Range.

On July 13, 1993, Doan family members and friends and the Dartmouth Outing Club trail crew gathered at the Smarts Mountain trailhead in Quinttown for the dedication of the Daniel Doan Trail, formerly the Mousley Brook Trail and at one time part of the Appalachian Trail. Dan himself was too ill to attend, but his words were present as Earl Jette, the director of Dartmouth College Outdoor Programs, read Dan's description of the hike from the first edition of *50 More Hikes in New Hampshire.* Then an orange DOC sign with the new trail name was nailed up. Dan was toasted with sparkling cider, and everybody sat down to a picnic.

At his home in Jefferson, New Hampshire, Dan took great delight in hearing the details of the ceremony, and he was deeply touched by the dedication, which was made "in recognition of Daniel Doan's efforts to stimulate interest and involvement in hiking and the out-of-doors."

Dan loved Smarts Mountain, the second mountain he climbed as a boy, after Cube. In the early editions of *50 More Hikes in New Hampshire,* he wrote a backpacking loop using this old trail along Mousley Brook to the summit for an overnight, then down via the Ranger Trail to the Lyme-Dorchester Road and back by the Quinttown Trail. "I'm a former Orford resident," he explained, "so I

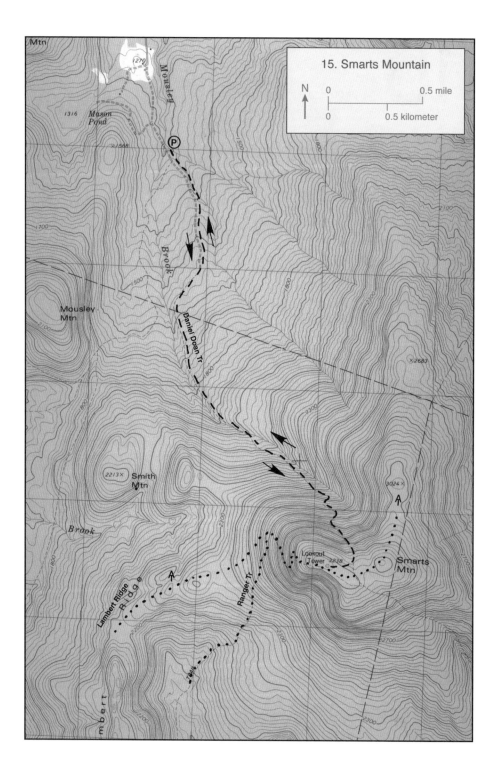

15. Smarts Mountain

naturally recommend the approach from that side, where the north slope rises from a valley of deserted farms known as Quinttown."

But in 1991 he decided he should change the loop to the more accessible trailhead in Lyme Center for the Lambert Ridge Trail and the Ranger Trail. This is the backpacking Hike 47 in the current *50 More Hikes in New Hampshire,* and in it Dan tells of his boyhood adventures on Smarts.

Now the trailhead in Quinttown is easier to find, thanks to clear road signs into this area of abandoned farms, where there is a pervading sense of the past that inspired Dan's novel *Amos Jackman,* set in a fictionalized Quinttown in the 1930s.

Dan's granddaughter, Thane Joyal, initiated an annual Daniel Doan Trail maintenance day, whose participants included Hal and Peggy Graham and other members of Trailwrights, members of the DOC, and Doan family and friends. James Munroe and Jason Berard are the trail co-adopters who take care of it the rest of the year. (If you are interested in volunteering to work on the trail, please get in touch with the DOC by going to www.dartmouth.edu/~doc/.)

The following description of the Daniel Doan Trail incorporates Dan's description from the early editions of *50 More Hikes in New Hampshire.*

HOW TO GET THERE

Coming from the east, turn off in Wentworth onto NH 25A. At about 10.5 miles, watch closely on the left for a road sign: QUINTTOWN ROAD. Coming from the west, take NH 25A at its junction with NH 10 in Orford, drive about 3.9 miles, and watch for the sign on your right.

Turn onto the Quinttown Road, which climbs southeast along the north bank of Jacob's Brook. There's no village at Quinttown now, and the old farmland—some of it

first cleared by Benjamin Quint, who served during the Revolution as a sailor under John Paul Jones—has largely returned to forest. What once was Quinttown is now just an intersection.

At 1.8 miles you'll see a sign for the Mousley Brook Road. Turn right, crossing a one-lane bridge. At a T-shaped fork in the road, you are facing the site of the former schoolhouse. Bear right. The road twists up steeply in a hairpin turn to the left and continues uphill through woods. Then it levels through open fields and pastures, with an old barn on the right and a great view of Smarts.

At 2.6 miles from NH 25A, you reach the small parking area on the left. Beware of a drop-off at the edge. There is an orange DOC sign for the Daniel Doan Trail.

THE TRAIL

At the start of the hike, you will be walking along a private driveway. If the gate across the driveway is closed, go around the gate. You come to two bridges, side by side. Take the bridge on the right. Continue straight ahead, ignoring a woods road to the right. Then you'll reach a junction, with a house on your left and the Daniel Doan Trail straight ahead, blazed blue.

For most of the first 2 miles the trail ascends gradually. This is an early farm road, as indicated by old apple trees and stone walls. These woods were open fields grown with brush when Dan first explored them. At a fork, take the trail to the right. Do not go left across a snowmobile bridge. At about 0.75 miles you come to a clearing on the right, and a logging road crosses the trail. Keep straight ahead.

You leave this area for higher valley forests along Mousley Brook. The logging done there over the years has apparently not disturbed the black bears, which probably now outnumber the people in Quinttown.

During the time of ripe shadbush berries, about the first week in August, bears leave tracks in the mud of the trail and break off branches from the small trees in greedy attempts to reach the berries. Don't worry about meeting a bear. He'll be long gone before you come anywhere near him. . . except perhaps after a rain, when the combination of quiet footing and a wind in your face might prevent your sounds and scent from preceding you.

At 1.5 miles, look for blue blazes on your left, where the trail bypasses a short eroded stretch. Take this bypass. The old trail will soon rejoin it, coming in on your right.

The logging road has kept to the north of Mousley Brook as far as the base of the mountain. There, at 1.9 miles, it crosses to the south bank and begins the real ascent. The climb alternates between short, steep sections and older, contour-following sled roads.

Trailwrights at Daniel Doan Trail DONALD K. MACDOUGALL

Finally you are climbing on a mountain trail over rocks and roots, which can be slippery. White birches give way to spruce and fir. Leveling, the trail swings right. It passes on log bridges over a boggy area draining from Murphy Spring. Boreal chickadees have a liking for these evergreen woods. You climb out of the spruces into a small clearing around the old fire warden's cabin.

Continue ahead to reach the summit and the fire tower hidden by spruces. From the tower you look across the Connecticut River valley to Vermont and can see Mount Ascutney southward, Killington and Pico to the southwest, and Camel's Hump and Mount Mansfield to the northwest. Turning to New Hampshire, you look north and east over nearby Mount Cube's quartzite-frosted summit. Then there are Mounts Carr, Stinson, Kineo, Moosilauke, the Franconia Range, and finally Washington.

Dan always looked northwest into Orford. He selected a domed hill called Sunday Mountain. (As a child, he thought it was so named because it was shaped like the scoop of ice cream in a sundae.) Then on its shoulder, Dame Hill, he located his first farm, where he raised chickens in the 1930s.

To the south, under the steep brow of the mountain, Reservoir Pond gleams. Cummins Pond lies to the east along the Lyme-Dorchester Road. To the southwest, there are the Dartmouth Skiway's slopes and lifts near Holt's Ledge, and farther south, Moose Mountain in Hanover.

After enjoying the view and your lunch, return to the Daniel Doan Trail for the descent. Shortly after crossing the brook, bear right at the bypass fork. Then continue on down to Quinttown.

Franconia Notch Region

The view pushed me. I sank down on a rock and tried to sort out some detail from the total wildness. The silent splendor was too simple for the word, just trees really, but it brought me a shiver.

–Daniel Doan,
Our Last Backpack

16

Artist's Bluff and Bald Mountain

Distance (round trip): 1½ miles
Walking time: 1¼ hours
Vertical rise: 600 feet
Maps: USDA/FS 7½' Franconia; USGS 7½' Franconia

Franconia Notch, with its state park and two lakes, the tramway, and ski trails, all bordering the I-93 parkway, has too many attractions for a quick visit. Don't try to see all the lakes, streams, and precipices in a day. Along with Cannon Mountain, Eagle Cliff, and Mount Lafayette, they are overpowering. First, get a hiker's perspective. If time is short and the urge to escape speeding cars and wandering tourists is imperative, climb Artist's Bluff and Bald Mountain at the north end of the notch. You need only an hour or two.

The most famous sight in Franconia Notch, the Old Man of the Mountain, collapsed in May 2003.

HOW TO GET THERE

Drive north on I-93's Franconia Notch Parkway past the tramway and its cable cars. Take Exit 34C onto NH 18. You can park at the Echo Lake Beach parking lot, but a fee is charged. To park free drive past the Echo Lake Beach parking area about 0.3 mile to the parking area for the Roland Peabody Memorial Slope. If this parking area is closed, park opposite it, off the road.

THE TRAIL

Walk back east along NH 18, just past the Echo Lake Beach parking lot. Or take the 0.4 mile path that runs between the Bald Mountain and Artist's Bluff trailheads. Its name used to be Short Circuit, and it is now called Loop Trail. Another name change may be coming soon, as there's a proposal for the Bald Mountain–Artist's Bluff Path to become

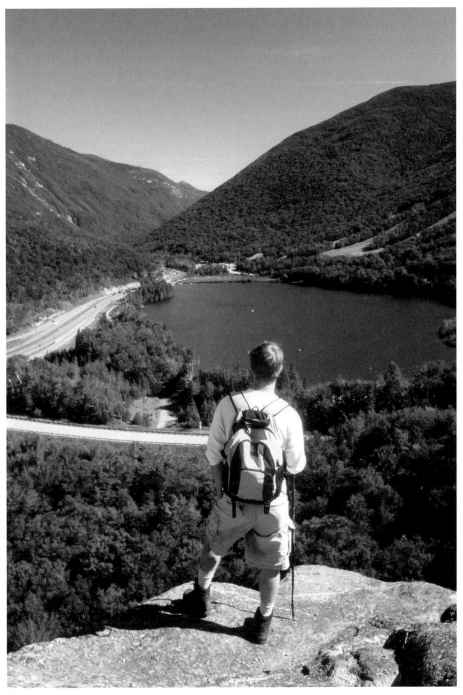

On Artist's Bluff

ROBERT J. KOZLOW

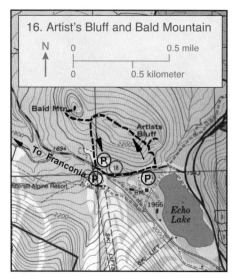

16. Artist's Bluff and Bald Mountain

the Veterans Trail in honor of New Hampshire's veterans.

The trail up Artist's Bluff starts on the north side of NH 18, on your left, west of the outlet from Echo Lake. Follow a path worn in the embankment gravel. The trail enters the woods and leads up among big rocks, with a very steep climb up a gully.

Near the top, at the junction with the trail to Bald Mountain, continue straight ahead on a spur trail a few yards to Artist's Bluff. This is a rock cliff from which artists might paint the notch, but it's more often a vantage point for photographers. The view is magnificent across Echo Lake to Eagle Cliff and Mount Lafayette on the left and to Cannon Mountain on the right.

For a complete hike above the northern and western gateways of the notch, return to the trail and turn right. Climb the remainder of the gully and over the wooded height above. The trail leads up and down over the knolls. You pass another ledge lookoff before you descend to the sag below Bald Mountain's summit. The trail joins a former carriage road up from NH 18. Turn right for the Bald Mountain spur trail. Be prepared to do some scrambling and to walk up bare ledges to reach the top.

On the rocky open summit at 2,340 feet, you stand clear of the small spruces. You look west over Franconia village, far away to the Connecticut River Valley, and into Vermont. Cannon Mountain's ski slopes are south. Turning around left, you look into the deep notch, again across Echo Lake.

Return to the junction with the Bald Mountain–Artist's Bluff Path. Turn right and follow the trail down the graded, ancient carriage road to NH 18 and your car.

Note: If you prefer descending a steep trail to ascending, do this hike in reverse, so that you will come down the trail from Artist's Bluff.

17

Mount Pemigewasset

Distance (round trip): 3½ miles

Walking time: 3 hours

Vertical rise: 1,250 feet

Maps: USDA/FS 7½' Lincoln; USGS 7½' Lincoln

Mount Pemigewasset, at the south end of Franconia Notch, is the buttress for the Indian Head, whose impassive profile looks down upon the motels and restaurants along old US 3 and to I-93 curving to the south. The summit's clifftop also has views of peaks far and near. The mountain extends north from the cliffs forming the Indian Head, and the trail to the top in that direction starts near the parking for the Flume Visitor Center. The open ledges at the end of the climb give the mountain an individuality that is more spectacular than its height would suggest, for its elevation is only 2,557 feet, less than half that of Mount Lafayette 5 miles away to the northeast.

After the tourist attractions of the notch, you'll be refreshed by this climb above the parkway and by the view of the mountains and valley. At sunset, you watch the horizon glow, and you are treated to a much rarer sight: the low-angled shadows and the brilliancy of the late sun on the peaks of the notch, a series of gleaming crests above the purple valley.

It will be time then to return to the highway and your car. For a sunset hike, take a headlamp or a flashlight with new batteries and a picnic supper in a small knapsack. If you linger on the mountain, you will find that the twilight of the summit has changed to darkness in the valley.

In the days of mountain inns, instead of returning to a parked car, you would have crossed a lawn to the lights and hospitality of the Flume House.

17. Mount Pemigewasset

HOW TO GET THERE

Take Exit 34A off I-93's Franconia Notch Parkway onto US 3. As you drive into the Flume Visitor Center, bear left to the north end parking area. The southern end of the Franconia Notch Bike Path is here. Leave your car and walk up the bike path 150 yards to a sign on the left for the Mount Pemigewasset Trail.

THE TRAIL

This gravel path soon takes you through an underpass below US 3. Turn left over a footbridge, and follow the trail through hardwoods to a second underpass, and then to

a third, completing your passage under the parkway. You might pause to admire the intricate stonework of granite facings on the concrete underpass.

Two hundred feet upward, you enter a forest of beech, maple, yellow birch, white birch, and other deciduous trees. The trail swings to the right and begins slabbing the contour, where it has been dug into the slope or provided with stone steps. You cross three small brooks on bridges of flattened logs. After the third log bridge, turn left up a steep rise. You are on the old trail that existed before the parkway and Flume Visitor Center.

Franconia Notch Region

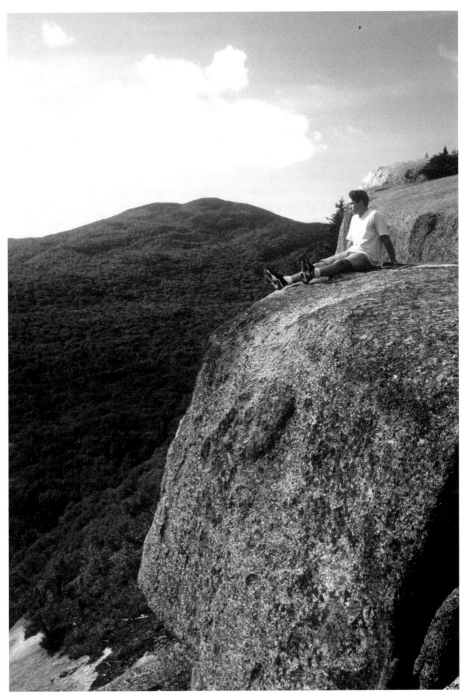

On Mount Pemigewasset

Here the climb really begins, but along a curving, moderate route among the great trunks of ancient beeches and maples. At one corner you will face a particularly massive beech. Look up at the claw marks in the smooth, gray bark. One fall, a black bear climbed up this tree to reach the beechnuts in the branches. Both large and small black bears have this urge and capability. Keep watching as you move on, and you may find other beeches with claw marks, although I doubt if you will find any recent, unhealed scars. Bears have five toes and five claws, yet usually only four show on the trees. The little toe on the inside of the paw (unlike the human toe arrangement) does not often dig into the bark.

Steady climbing lifts you to the north side of the mountain in a growth of spruce and fir. The Indian Head Trail comes in on your right; continue ahead. The almost level trail follows for a short distance the edge of a wooded drop-off on your right. Three yards of upward scramble put you into a green tunnel with a stone floor. On a good day, you emerge with blinking eyes into bright sunlight. The slanting ledge ends in emptiness and distant mountains. With trees at your back you are standing beside the scalp lock of the Indian Head. Here is the place to bring wandering children under control.

The view immediately ahead below the cliff is one of both forest and human enterprise. To the right, a leafy forest turns brilliant yellow, red, and orange in early October. It stretches away to a swampy area along Harvard Brook known as Bog Eddy. Beyond this, and bearing northwest, you see the cut of a power line, then farther away the triangular shape of Mount Wolf. The Kinsman Ridge Trail traverses that mountain as a section of the Appalachian Trail. The long ridge to the southwest is Mount Moosilauke, the westernmost of the White Mountains.

Looking to your left you'll see the ski trails on Loon Mountain east of Lincoln. Beyond and to the right is Mount Tecumseh; to the left, Mount Osceola, now without a fire tower. Together they form the north wall of Waterville Valley. For a complete eastern view, follow the ledge in that direction, keeping along the fringe of evergreens on your left.

Walk upward to the left and step onto the lookout ledge for the Franconia Range. From the south, the peaks are as follows: pointed Mount Flume and its massive slide; then somewhat nearer Mount Liberty, with its stepped rock summit; next Little Haystack Mountain, all rock and sun and cloud shadows. Below it is the top of the vast rock sheet called Shining Cliff, so very visible from Lafayette Place. The next is Mount Lincoln. Then comes the highest of them all, Mount Lafayette, and just to the left, the dome of North Lafayette.

Franconia Notch appears as walls of rock framing distant sky. The walls are Eagle Cliff to the right and the rock-climbers' playground, the expanse of cliffs on Cannon Mountain. The summit of Cannon Mountain is capped by the little block of the tram terminal.

Pointed evergreens in front of you form delicate ornamentation against the panorama—and in time may grow up to obscure it. At present, the green tips give the view a truly northern setting; a final reward before you turn around and descend the way you came.

18

Basin-Cascades Trail

Distance (to Cascade Brook Trail and back): 2½ miles

Walking time: 2 hours

Vertical rise: 550 feet

Maps: USDA/FS 7½' Lincoln; USGS 7½' Lincoln; USDA/FS 7½' Franconia; USGS 7½' Franconia

Of the various trails maintained in Franconia Notch by the New Hampshire Division of Parks and Recreation, the Basin-Cascades Trail is one of the most interesting. It passes through woods of fine stature and climbs up beside falls, pools, and rock formations along the way.

The Basin-Cascades Trail may be considered a link from the Basin to Cascade Brook Trail, which leads on to Lonesome Lake. But for hikers exploring the notch it is an experience in itself for an afternoon in mountain woods.

HOW TO GET THERE

If you're driving north on I-93's Franconia Notch Parkway, the exit for the Basin is about 6 miles beyond Exit 32 to Lincoln. Heading south, you'll see the Basin exit about 3.6 miles from Cannon Mountain.

THE TRAIL

For the Basin-Cascades Trail, turn back from the viewing area, cross a footbridge over a tributary stream, and enter the woods on a gravel path. Avoid taking paths to the left or right. Your trail's sign appears just beyond a right fork to another bridge and a path across a little hollow to a sign for the Pemi Trail. (The Pemi Trail leads north 1.5 miles along the west side of the river to Lafayette Place.) The Basin-Cascades Trail bears left after its sign, which is about 250 feet from the Basin.

At a slight incline, you approach the north bank of Cascade Brook. Blue-blazed, the trail steepens and is often rough, laced by

18. Basin-Cascades Trail

N

0   0.25 mile

0   0.25 kilometer

exposed roots, and at times muddy. The much-worn path branches with informal spurs to the left for views where the brook slides over smooth ledges.

Signs on trees announce that you are at the boundary of the White Mountain National Forest and consequently will leave behind the Franconia Notch State Park. The history of the park explains why you are hiking in such a magnificent forest. In the 1920s these trees very nearly fell to the logger's ax and saw. The Society for the Protection of New Hampshire Forests aroused people to the danger. A donation of a dollar bought a tree in the society's campaign "Buy a Tree and Help Save the Notch." Major contributions came in from philanthropists, who would now be called conservationists or environmentalists. Women's clubs, newspapers, and the AMC contributed, as did

     Franconia Notch Region

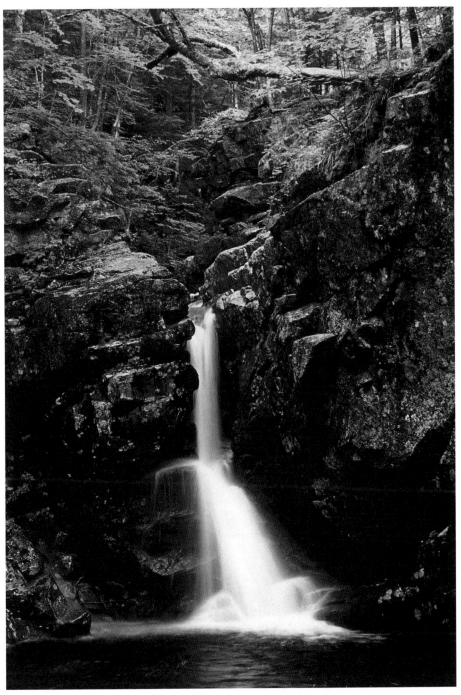

Kinsman Falls

New Hampshire taxpayers through their legislature, which appropriated half the $400,000 required to buy the 6,000 acres along 7 miles of Route 3. On September 15, 1928, the Old Man of the Mountain overlooked the preservation ceremonies held at Profile Lake. The park was dedicated to the New Hampshire men and women who had served the nation in time of war.

Continuing up into the national forest, the Basin-Cascades Trail becomes less steep but remains just as rough. Keep uphill under fine hemlocks to Kinsman Falls. After rain, this cascade through chutes in the rock is a broad sheet of water sluicing over a vast expanse of smooth granite. Below the falls the trail crosses the brook on rocks. The crossing may be dangerous at high water. Under any conditions it may deter casual adult walkers and families with small children.

Across the brook, the blazes change to yellow, then back to blue. The trail climbs steeply and continues to follow the brook through evergreen woods. Scrambling in places is necessary. Tree roots have been exposed by erosion and boots. The spruces shadow the brook so that Rocky Glen Falls appears as a glistening in the branches ahead. Keep left at the base of the falls, and enter a chasm with damp rock walls. When you climb out of it and bear right you are above the falls and again beside the brook. A few yards farther on your left you pass the broken timbers of a footbridge. Soon you reach the end of the Basin-Cascade Trail at its junction with the Cascade Brook Trail.

Day hikers with the time and energy to visit Lonesome Lake may follow Cascade Brook Trail, but there is no bridge, and at high water the crossing can be dangerous. Follow Cascade Brook Trail 1.5 miles to the lake and the AMC hut there. (See Hike 19.)

Those who turn back from such a long round-trip of 5.5 miles can enjoy the descent along the same Basin-Cascades Trail, saving the excursion to Lonesome Lake for another day. Returning on the trail you've been ascending shows you the woods and streams in a different light and perspective, so in a sense it becomes another trail. Cascade Brook rushing down the mountainside may not seem to be plunging toward the sea, but it surely is, and will return as water vapor in clouds to again drench these mountains and replenish this lovely brook.

19

Lonesome Lake

Distance (round trip): 3¼ miles
Walking time: 2¾ hours
Vertical rise: 1,000 feet
Maps: USDA/FS 7½' Franconia; USGS 7½' Franconia

One thousand feet above Franconia Notch is Lonesome Lake, a goal for climbers and visitors who take advantage of the graded trail to walk in and see a true mountain lake in a spectacular setting. No longer "lonesome," it's quite the opposite. The much-used trails, along with the AMC hut and the hikers with their colorful packs and clothes, give a modern touch to the ancient scenery.

The lake has been popular since the days of mountain inns after the Civil War. The Lonesome Lake Trail still mostly follows the old bridle path, along which many vacationers from the now-vanished hotels rode to the lake for the magnificent view of the mountains on both sides of the notch.

Legend names President Ulysses S. Grant as one of the notable visitors. According to the story, he came to the notch and the Profile House in 1869. A yellow coach and six bay horses driven by Ed Cox, a famous "whip," brought him from Bethlehem in 55 minutes—a fantastic rate of more than 13 miles an hour. In later years, a steam train and rails brought guests to the Profile House, which burned in August 1923.

The views from Lonesome Lake are, indeed, great—comprehensive, craggy, wild, and dominated by the treeless peak of Mount Lafayette. From the lake, trails lead to Cannon Mountain, Kinsman Mountain, and Kinsman Pond. The Appalachian Trail passes by the lower end of the lake.

The AMC's Lonesome Lake Hut is situated on the west shore facing the Franconia Range. There is a trail around the lake, 0.75 mile, passing the site of old log cabins. A

19. Lonesome Lake

stand of tamarack makes a fine display of yellow in the fall. The lake is 2,734 feet above sea level. Westward, the evergreen forest rises to the ledges of Kinsman Mountain.

HOW TO GET THERE

Your destination is the Lafayette Place Campground. Northbound on I-93's Franconia Notch Parkway, note your mileage as you pass Exit 34A. Continue on the parkway about 4 miles to an exit sign: TRAILHEAD PARKING. Smaller signs list the Bridle Path and Falling Waters Trail, but this exit is also for the Lonesome Lake Trail.

Leave your car in the parking area, and walk through the foot tunnel under the parkway to the west side. When you emerge from the tunnel, bear left around the log cabin. Farther on you'll see a sign on your right for the Lonesome Lake Trailhead. Continue to the end of the south parking area.

(Driving north on the parkway, you will see a sign before the Trailhead Parking exit that tells you to take the Tramway exit, 34B, for the Lafayette Place Campground. If you plan to head south after your hike, you may want to park at this campground instead of in the east side trailhead parking area.)

If you are heading south on I-93's Franconia Notch Parkway, take the exit for the Lafayette Place Campground and Trailhead Parking, about 2 miles south of Exit 34B for the Cannon Mountain Tramway.

THE TRAIL

The Lonesome Lake Trail begins with a footbridge over a brook, which is the infancy of the Pemigewasset River. Follow yellow blazes and signs past the campsites. Leaving the campground behind, you proceed into the forest of tall hardwoods.

No-strain climbing limbers your legs. Not far beyond a left corner and two small bridges, you pass by the Hi-Cannon Trail on your right. This is about 0.5 mile from your car. Now the trail lifts you upward by the switchbacks originally designed for horses and riders. You may note the slope's steepness and welcome the angling path that you follow. The ridge, which looked so easy from Lafayette Place, seems to have deceived you. But the trail soon begins to level out, and after about 1 mile you detect a slight descent. The lake is ahead in its flat, wooded setting. You come to a trail junction. Pause here and study the trail sign and the numerous trails listed. Orient yourself to the map. Even look behind you to familiarize yourself with the trail you've been on so you'll recognize it when you return.

To reach the AMC hut, take the Cascade Brook Trail, which branches left from the Lonesome Lake Trail. Follow along the east shore of the lake until you come to another trail junction at the lake's south end. Turn right on the Fishin' Jimmy Trail across the outlet, and take the left fork to the AMC hut.

For the return route, walk the Around-Lonesome-Lake Trail on the west shore to a junction with the Lonesome Lake Trail north of the lake. Turn right. Keep past the Cascade Brook Trail, and you are on the way back down to Lafayette Place.

Lonesome Lake

ROBERT J. KOZLOW

20

Mount Flume

Distance (round trip): 10 miles
Walking time: 8 hours
Vertical rise: 3,367 feet
Maps: USDA/FS 7½' Lincoln; USGS 7½' Lincoln

Appearing as a rocky pinnacle to drivers and passengers northbound on I-93 and US 3 beyond North Woodstock, Mount Flume sets the style for the Franconia Range. This southern terminus of the long ridge above treeline is a fitting introduction to Mount Liberty, Mount Lincoln, and Mount Lafayette. But Mount Flume has its own distinction: namely, its rock slides and exposed ledges. These and the trail to the summit for this hike—the Flume Slide Trail—require a brief explanation.

Perhaps you have turned into the Flume Visitor Center for information and for a careful view of this mountain. From the parking area you may stare aghast at the obviously impossible face of the peak. Despite the trail's name it surely can't lead up that. It doesn't—not exactly. The name refers to an earlier slide off to the right, now mostly hidden in trees that have grown on the original gash. It's formidable enough, however, so don't visit the famous Flume Gorge on the same day you hike. And take into consideration the challenges of this demanding hike, which has a very steep and potentially dangerous climb up rock faces. Also, do the hike as described here, a loop from Mount Flume to Mount Liberty; do not descend the Flume Slide Trail.

Note: Many hikers now prefer to take the relocated Osseo Trail, via the Lincoln Woods Trail, to Mount Flume. It is longer, about 11 miles round trip, but pleasant, with an excellent view into the Pemigewasset Wilderness from a shoulder on the approach to the ridge.

HOW TO GET THERE

Take Exit 34A off I-93's Franconia Notch Parkway onto US 3. As you drive into the Flume Visitor Center, bear left to the north end parking area.

THE TRAIL

At a sign saying BEGIN BIKE ROUTE, follow the asphalt bike path for about 20 minutes or take the Whitehouse Trail, which branches off the bike path on the left and rejoins in 0.75 mile before reaching the bridge over the Pemigewasset River. Here the Cascade Brook Trail joins from the left. Beyond the bridge, watch on the right for the Liberty Spring Trail 200 feet farther along. You leave the bike path at this point.

The Liberty Spring Trail, a section of the Appalachian Trail, takes you up fairly steeply through a leafy forest, and in 0.5 mile to a sidehill fork. Keep right onto the Flume Slide

Trail. (The Liberty Spring Trail continues toward the Liberty Spring Campsite and Mount Liberty. It will be the lower section of your return route.)

Taking the Flume Slide Trail from this junction, you begin a woods walk south and east for almost 3 miles to the base of the mountain. The trail follows a series of old logging roads and crosses various tributaries of Flume Brook. As it approaches the base of the slide, the trail can be altered annually by spring freshets, so watch for the blue blazes.

The challenge of Mount Flume begins at the slide. For more than 0.5 mile, you face the side of the mountain where once an avalanche of rocks and gravel poured down. Now grown to small birches and evergreens, it still keeps your eyes focused on footholds and handholds. *Caution is required.* You will encounter several sections of open rock slabs that demand

On Mount Flume, looking toward Mount Liberty   ROBERT J. KOZLOW

attention on sunny days and are treacherous in rain. It may take you an hour and a half to do this 0.5 mile in good weather.

Pause for the views opening across the notch to Kinsman Mountain and Cannon Mountain.

At the top of the slide keep left as the trail enters spruces and firs, climbing to the junction with the Franconia Ridge Trail. At the right, the Osseo Trail leads south and east to the Lincoln Woods Trail and the Kancamagus Highway 5.5 miles away.

Follow the Franconia Ridge Trail left, up into the spruce scrub, to the edge of the open cliffs that you saw from the Flume Visitor Center. The trail skirts the edge, not a good route for anyone troubled by heights, although the scrub on the right can comfort and assist. A few yards north is the summit of the peak, a small area of rock. The effect is immediate: a sense of achievement and emergence from a hard climb to an extreme

height, elevation 4,328 feet. The panorama is grand in all directions.

Northward you see the barren and rocky crests of Mount Liberty, Mount Lincoln, and Mount Lafayette, highest in the range. Turning west, you look across the notch to the humped summits of Kinsman Mountain, and, at the head of the notch, Cannon Mountain bulking above the cliffs. To the east, your eyes sweep over the forested valleys draining into the Pemigewasset River's East Branch. The far ridge in the Pemigewasset Wilderness rises north from cliffs to Mount Bond's treeless summit. Mount Carrigain, farther east, bounds the wilderness with its massive pyramid topped by an observation tower.

Continue on to Mount Liberty, down and up about 1.1 miles north along the Franconia Ridge Trail. Beyond the peak, turn left down the Liberty Spring Trail and descend to the Whitehouse Trail for completion of the loop back to your car. (See Hike 21, Mount Liberty.)

21

Mount Liberty

Distance (round trip): 7½ miles

Walking time: 6 hours

Vertical rise: 3,100 feet

Maps: USDA/FS 7½' Lincoln; USGS 7½' Lincoln

The ledgy crest of Mount Liberty lines up with the higher Franconia Range northward and provides closer views of the notch from a better angle than Mount Flume. Instead of a slide for a final approach, the Liberty Spring Trail leads up past a tentsite popular with Appalachian Trail hikers.

A day pack with suitable equipment is necessary. The topmost crags can be cold and windy.

HOW TO GET THERE

The climb, like the one up Mount Flume (see Hike 20), begins at the Flume Visitor Center. Take Exit 34A off I-93's Franconia Notch Parkway onto US 3. As you drive into the Flume Visitor Center, bear left to the north end parking area.

THE TRAIL

At a sign reading BEGIN BIKE ROUTE, follow the asphalt bike path for about 20 minutes or take the Whitehouse Trail, which branches off the bike path on the left and rejoins in 0.75 mile before reaching the bridge over the Pemigewasset River. Here the Cascade Brook Trail joins from the left. Beyond the bridge, watch on the right for the Liberty Spring Trail 200 feet farther on.

The Liberty Spring Trail leads you along a short level section before you start the 0.5-mile climb to the fork where Flume Slide Trail branches right. Keep left, as the Liberty Spring Trail continues up through the hardwood forest and crosses a brook. When water is high, this crossing may be difficult.

21. Mount Liberty

Steadily rising, the trail takes you up slopes once logged and burned. In 1917, hikers climbing among rocks scorched bare by a forest fire followed signs nailed to blackened stubs.

The trail swings up steeply to your right, then becomes more gradual and passes Liberty Spring Tentsite. (No shelter here; tent platforms only. Last water.) On up through the spruce/fir woods you climb to the Franconia Ridge Trail. Turn right (south) and follow the Franconia Ridge Trail up into the open, where you see the steep rocky summit ahead. You feel that lift of excitement from the expanse of sky and mountain, and from the certainty that you'll soon surmount the last rocks.

This 4,459-foot peak overlooks the great forests to the east in the Pemigewasset Wilderness. Northward, along the Franconia Ridge Trail, your gaze adjusts to the increasing height beyond Little Haystack Mountain, where narrow ledges rise to Mount Lincoln. On the left a distant green ridge curves down from the AMC's Greenleaf Hut into the notch below Mount Lafayette, which Mount Lincoln obscures. North, across the notch, the high cliffs of Cannon Mountain appear chopped from the wooded summit. Westward, Kinsman Mountain's slope and long summit ridge parallel the highway. In the opposite direction, east, Owl's Head, more like a great whale, fills the valley north toward Mount Garfield. Over Owl's Head, past

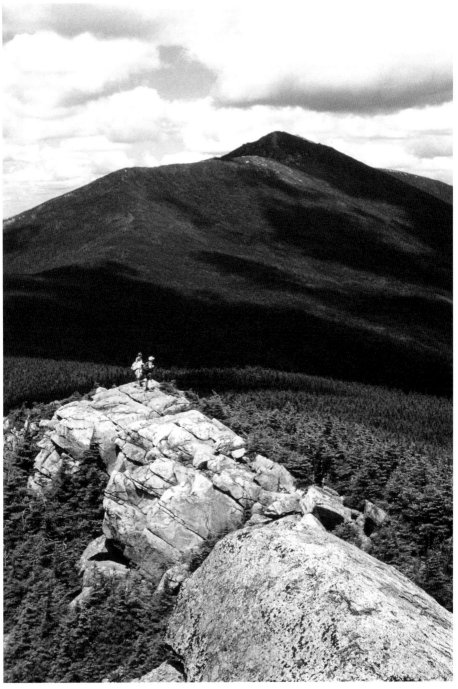

On Mount Liberty, looking toward Franconia Ridge Trail

ROBERT J. KOZLOW

Mount Guyot, the peak on the northeast horizon is Mount Washington. And all around, distant under a clear sky and high clouds, the mountains seem endless.

Often, however, Mount Liberty is in cloud, and the wind is cold. But luck favors the prepared hiker. If you carry plenty of extra clothing and a rain parka in your pack, maybe you won't need them; then you can sit in the sun and enjoy your sandwiches.

The descent takes you north along the Franconia Ridge Trail on the same route you climbed. Turn left onto the Liberty Spring Trail, and continue to the bike path and the Whitehouse Trail, which you follow back to your car.

22

Mount Lincoln

Distance (round trip, Mount Lincoln only): 8 miles; (around the loop, Lincoln and Lafayette): 8¾ miles

Walking time (Mount Lincoln only): 5¾ hours; (around the loop): 7½ hours

Vertical rise (to Mount Lincoln): 3,350 feet; (around the loop): 3,750 feet*

Maps: USDA/FS 7½' Franconia; USGS 7½' Franconia

*Mount Lafayette is only 171 feet higher than Mount Lincoln, but the climb from the col north of Mount Lincoln is 400 feet.

To many hikers along the Franconia Ridge Trail, Mount Lincoln is a way station on the high line of peaks knifing north and south above Franconia Notch east of I-93. But Mount Lincoln can be a fine destination in itself. During the ascent, you will see spectacular waterfalls; a unique slanting cliff; an alpine-arctic environment above treeline; and wide, wide views, especially overlooking the Pemigewasset Wilderness, clear away to Crawford Notch and Mount Washington. This hike offers the added bonus, if you wish, of a climb up the highest peak in the Franconia Range, Mount Lafayette.

HOW TO GET THERE

Driving north on I-93's Franconia Notch Parkway, note your mileage as you pass Exit 34A. Continue on the parkway for an additional 4 miles to an exit with signs for Trailhead Parking, Bridle Path, and Falling Waters Trail. If you are driving south on the parkway, take the exit for the Lafayette Place Campground and Trailhead Parking, about 2 miles south of Exit 34B for the Cannon Mountain Tramway. A pedestrian underpass connects parking on either side of the parkway. This hike starts at the east or northbound parking area.

THE TRAIL

Your trails for this hike leave the east parking area to the left of the hiker information kiosk. The Old Bridle Path and the Falling Waters Trail coincide for 0.2 mile. At the bridge over Walker Brook they separate. Turn right across the brook onto the Falling

22. Mount Lincoln

N
0   0.5 mile

0   0.5 kilometer

Waters Trail. You leave this stream, which flows from a ravine of the same name on Mount Lafayette. (The Old Bridle Path keeps straight for a short distance before bearing left to join the route it took before the parkway was constructed. If you choose the loop for this hike, the Old Bridle Path will be your descent trail.)

Along the Falling Waters Trail you ascend gradually, swinging through woods of maple, beech, and yellow birch for another 0.5 mile to Dry Brook. Contrary to its name, the brook is a crystal torrent in early summer.

You cross Dry Brook to the south bank and begin a steeper climb. You pass Stairs Falls cascade and approach ledges high up in the trees. The trail appears to end at a pool in a narrow ravine. Swiftwater Falls gushes into the pool from a ledge 60 feet high. You see the trail to the left of the falls. You cross to the opposite bank over rocks at the foot of the pool.

The climb begins here in earnest, although the trail is graded, and sections of it follow old logging roads. You were impressed by Swiftwater Falls. Now Cloudland Falls, 20 feet higher, descends toward you in a white, shifting curtain sliding into the gorge.

Above Cloudland Falls, from the steep and slippery ledge, you first look out across the valley. Then you cross to the south bank and cross back to the north bank. The trail continues up, rough and steep as the brook branches into the upper growth of spruce and fir. The trail takes you up a series of traverses between steeper pitches to a left turn at a junction. Here a spur trail to the right leads 100 yards down to the base of Shining Rock Cliff. This massive expanse of smooth granite angles up at a rounded 45 degrees for 200 feet to your left. It extends four times that distance across the ridge. It gleams in the sun when wet from the drainage off its brow of evergreens. Don't try to climb it. From your parked car at Lafayette Place in late afternoon you can see it really shining.

Back at the junction with the main trail you may wonder how much farther it is to the alpine-arctic environment I promised you. In the next 0.5 mile the trail clears the scrub of treeline in a steep ascent into the open rockery of Little Haystack, a minor peak on the Franconia Ridge Trail.

If the wind blows rain, and clouds are settling into a blinding fog, this is a good place to turn back. Wait for a better day. The exciting panorama from the ridge demands a clear view. There's no value in a memory of Mount Lincoln as gray rocks packed in cotton batting. Besides, the ridge is dangerous in stormy weather. Lightning strikes frequently. Winds can be icy, even in summer.

Franconia Ridge Trail from Mount Lafayette   ROBERT J. KOZLOW

You will be almost a mile up in the sky. The col between Little Haystack and Mount Lincoln is exposed, narrow, and in places almost sheer on each side.

In fine weather, turn north along the Franconia Ridge Trail and enjoy the 0.75 mile above trees in the open exposure of sun and sky. The summit of Mount Lincoln is at 5,089 feet.

Multiplicities of mountains rise in all directions, and on the east the rocks fall away to green forests along Lincoln Brook and Franconia Brook, which flow around 4,025-foot Owl's Head, anchored like a humped barge in the green sea of trees.

For a loop that will return you to your car, the Franconia Ridge Trail provides a clear-day bonus. North, beyond Mount Lincoln's summit, the trail descends over and among rocks, all in the open, then up to Mount Lafayette's rugged slopes and summit cairn— a 1-mile hike among alpine-arctic plants, such as diapensia, hugging the windswept ledges. From Mount Lafayette, turn left and go down by the Greenleaf Trail to the AMC's Greenleaf Hut. Then take the Old Bridle Path for the descent along a ridge where, in June, the rhodora blossoms are showy pink above Walker Ravine. The Old Bridle Path takes you to the junction with the Falling Waters Trail at the bridge over Walker Brook and then to the east parking. If you don't choose to include the loop to Mount Lafayette, you may return from Mount Lincoln as you climbed and enjoy once again Shining Rock Cliff, Cloudland Falls, and Swiftwater Falls.

23

Mount Lafayette

Distance (round trip): 7¾ miles

Walking time: 7 hours

Vertical rise: 3,400 feet

Maps: USDA/FS 7½' Franconia; USGS 7½' Franconia

The "top of the world" in the Franconia Range is, of course, named for the French hero of the American Revolution, the Marquis de Lafayette. His 1825 visit to New Hampshire brought about the change from the peak's older name of Great Haystack. Its northwestern cliffs and slides form the east side of Franconia Notch above Profile Lake. Its long, forested slopes of beech, yellow and white birch, and maple rise steeply from the parkway. Far up among the spruce scrub and barren rocks of treeline are two small lakes and the Greenleaf Hut of the AMC. The dwarf trees and ledges extend to a rock-strewn slope, 1 mile long, leading up to the summit at 5,260 feet, with rare mosses, plants, lichens, and grasses along the way.

The exposed stones of the peak could be in the arctic rather than the temperate zone. Even on a summer day the wind often blows bitter cold. Plants are balanced on a delicate ecological margin. The dwarf spruces lie down before the wind and seem to grasp the rocks. Although doused with rain and fog, the mountain cranberry and similar creeping plants are thick-leaved against dehydration from the wind. The leaves of the low shrub, Labrador tea, curl along the edges and are woolly underneath, thereby retarding evaporation of vital leaf moisture in the harsh winds. These mountain vines, prostrate bushes, and shrubby heaths blossom white, pink, and purple in early summer.

Mount Lafayette has long been a popular climb. The oldest trail, still called the Old Bridle Path, was more than a name once. Travelers rode up it on mountain ponies from

23. Mount Lafayette

N

0		0.5 mile
0		0.5 kilometer

nearby inns. There were two inns in the notch named Lafayette. The Lafayette House was built about 1835 where the Profile House later stood, in the vicinity of the present-day Cannon Mountain Tramway. The Mount Lafayette House came later, about 1850, and was situated near the area now known as Lafayette Campground (see Hike 25, Cannon Mountain). The Mount Lafayette House burned in 1861. Only foundation stones remain of the summit house, too, which in those days accommodated the successful climbers.

When the AMC built Greenleaf Hut in 1929, burros bore loads up the path and each year continued to transport supplies early in the season. Then, before the days of helicopters, the regular summer packing of necessary food and fuel depended on the legs and lungs of the hutmen lugging the long packboards. Still today, you will see "croo" members treading upward under heavy loads.

The Old Bridle Path, leaving the parkway from the east side at Lafayette Place, is the scenic route up Lafayette. The views of the upper ridge and of Walker Ravine open out from a partially wooded shoulder halfway up to Greenleaf Hut. Starting as it does at the same point as the Falling Waters Trail, described in the Mount Lincoln climb, the Old Bridle Path forms a pleasant and easy link in that loop. (See Hike 22.)

A northerly and more challenging route from Franconia Notch up Mount Lafayette, the Greenleaf Trail mounts beside Eagle Cliff and reaches the north slope through Eagle Pass, 1,000 feet above the notch.

HOW TO GET THERE
Driving I-93's Franconia Notch Parkway, take Exit 34B for the Cannon Mountain Tramway. Park at the south end of the parking area for the tram. You'll see a Greenleaf Trail sign. The trail is blazed blue.

THE TRAIL

With above-treeline equipment in your pack, follow the sidewalk back to the parkway and through the underpass. Turn left up the exit road, and then cross it to the sign for Greenleaf Hut on your right.

Climb the bank into the growth of hardwoods, and at once swing to the right as the trail begins a slabbing route south, parallel to the parkway, across the tailings of a slide. Soon, farther on, you continue on the trail that before 1987 began nearer Profile Lake.

Follow the blue blazes up a steeper section to a left turn and a series of switchbacks. Then the trail bears right. The footing is excellent and continues so on the upper trail as it curves north into Eagle Pass. You enter the pass under a long cliff similar to those towering still higher above. You pick your way over massive rocks as large as cottages, which have lodged in the pass. Snow and ice linger late in the gloomy caves below the boulders. If you leave the trail to explore, watch out for treacherous patches of moss over the crevices. The trail itself is safe enough.

Beyond the rocky confines of Eagle Pass, the trail turns sharply right and up moderately among slabs and imbedded flat rocks. The forest is mostly evergreens mixed with white birch and mountain ash. The trail zigzags to ease the steepness, along with occasional stone steps and waterbars. You are climbing a ridge high above Lafayette Brook on

Greenleaf Hut

your left. Across the ravine an opening in the trees gives a glimpse of a towering dome—North Lafayette. The grade remains steady to steeper switchbacks.

Then the trail enters a nearly level corridor in scrub. You step out behind Greenleaf Hut and look beyond to the open views and alpine barrens above treeline, east to the summit. The glacial age is long gone, but the ice scoured the rocks before it melted away, leaving great shards scattered precariously, a random and extravagant use of paving stone to wonder at.

Near the hut, the Old Bridle Path joins the Greenleaf Trail. You descend beyond the hut to the dwarf spruces again, then pass through the moist section at the little bog draining from the two basins of the Eagle Lakes. You climb above treeline once more and follow the worn pathway over the rocks. Massive cairns mark the route, which swings north for the final ascent.

If there's a storm brewing, turn around and leave the mountain to the lightning and thunder. If there's a clear hour ahead, watch the high clouds and their shadows moving across the mountains. Don't try to count the peaks. There are too many. Look east at the miles of green trees, and remember that before the days of the national forest, the valleys were a blackened devastation of logged and burned ridges.

Return by the same route, the Greenleaf Trail, turning right, north, at the hut for the descent to Eagle Pass.

24

North Lafayette

Distance (round trip): 9 miles

Walking time: 7½ hours

Vertical rise: 3,360 feet

Maps: USDA/FS 7½' Franconia; USGS 7½' Franconia

After you've surmounted (and recovered from?) the highest and most popular climbing summit in the Franconia Range—Mount Lafayette—a very different day awaits you on its north shoulder. From a rocky dome, sometimes called North Lafayette, you'll gaze at Mount Lafayette to the south half a mile away and in a rarely seen perspective across a wide bowl of rock slabs and talus. A remoteness from the crowd on North Lafayette's barren summit will emphasize the vastness of the mountain. You may even savor a mood of detachment, of isolation, which is a bonus for climbing this peak.

Of course it's not really isolated. The Garfield Ridge Trail crosses it at an elevation of about 5,080 feet. (The Garfield Ridge Trail traverses north from Mount Lafayette to the AMC's Galehead Hut, a difficult 6.5 miles of the Appalachian Trail.) This trail above treeline, with its white AT blazes, will be your final 0.25 mile southward after hiking 4.5 miles up the Skookumchuck Trail from US 3.

HOW TO GET THERE

The Skookumchuck Trail begins from the east side of US 3 at a parking area for the north end of the Franconia Notch Bike Path. Approaching from the south, drive through the notch on the Franconia Notch Parkway. Beyond the transition to I-93, take Exit 35 for US 3, and park on the right in 0.6 mile. Southbound on US 3, drive 0.25 mile past the junction of NH 141, and the trailhead will be to your left.

THE TRAIL

The trail leads into the woods from the north corner of the asphalt. Blue blazes mark the

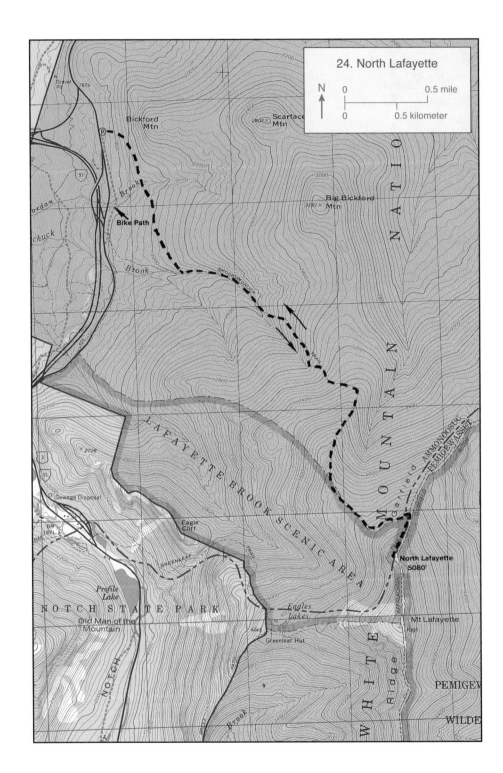

N

0   0.5 mile

0   0.5 kilometer

Gravel
Pit   1674

Bickford
Mtn

Scarface
Mtn
2802

Big Bickford
Mtn
3261

93

Bike Path

Brook

Brook

Brook

Brook

chuck

Jordan

SHOOKUMCHUCK

Trail

N A T I O

M O U N T A I N

Garfield

AMMONOOSUC

PEMIGEWASSET

L A F A Y E T T E   B R O O K   S C E N I C   A R E A

2728

Sewage Disposal

BM
1971

93

Eagle
Cliff

GREENLEAF

TRAIL

Profile
Lake

N O T C H   S T A T E   P A R K

Old Man of the
Mountain

Eagles
Lakes
4245

Greenleaf Hut

North Lafayette
5080'

Mt Lafayette
High

W
H
I
T
E

Ridge

GREENLEAF

NOTCH

PEMIGEW

Brook

WILDE

uphill for 100 yards to a curve southward. At 0.1 mile, the trail crosses a snowmobile trail. Ascending moderately before leveling off, the Skookumchuck Trail remains within hearing distance of I-93 traffic, whose roar diminishes gradually as the trail bears southeast. Still marked by blue blazes, the trail crosses a second branch of the snowmobile trail before crossing a small brook. It continues up and down over several seasonal trickles. Soon you look into a little valley and hear the rippling of Skookumchuck Brook. The trail descends at a long slant to join the old trail leading upstream along the north bank. This completes your traverse of the section necessitated by I-93 construction. You are 1.1 miles from your car.

Skookumchuck Brook, flowing steadily in its green valley, is very satisfying to walk beside. The original trail, gouged into the sidehill with log corduroy and crude bridges, tested one's ability to judge the depth of mud. In 1979 crews added stepping stones and split-log walkways. The bank on your left becomes higher and steeper as you walk, making you suspect a stiff scramble out. About 50 minutes from your car, the trail turns left and goes at the steep bank. For 300 feet you climb on rock steps. Deep waterbars of logs and earth prevent erosion. At the top your legs cease straining as the trail becomes less demanding. You reach another grade, which remains from the days of horse-drawn logging sleds. Spruces begin to blend with the white birches. Another steep climb brings you to a little flat, where a trickle of water drips from the slope on your right.

The trail bears right to the foot of another upward pitch—again with rock steps to aid you. Many large rocks hold the steep hillside in place and over time have become part of the landscape. You may wonder at their size because they sometimes require very high lifting of your boots, with knees approaching your chin. This is not due to a wry sense of humor

among trail crews. The rocks must weigh enough to hold them in the shallow earth.

At the top of the steps you begin a steady climb. Here the trail narrows, but the water-bars are adequate and the footing is good and not too rocky. The trees grow smaller. Approaching treeline? Not so. After a green tunnel 10 feet high, the larger birches reappear among tall evergreens and mountain ash trees. The trail slants downward, then continues through the corridor of evergreens, their cool shade broken by the bright sunlight in areas of spruce/fir blowdowns. Look up to your left and catch a glimpse of North Lafayette. It's not as far away as it appears.

The trail becomes typical of older routes on steep ridges. Evergreen branches reach into the narrow, rocky track and brush against your arms and hips. You grasp here and there tough roots or corners of rocks. Several short levels alternate with abrupt upward rock-scrambles till you leave behind the final stunted spruces and stand in the open at treeline. Cairns mark the way up to the junction with the Garfield Ridge Trail.

Turn right onto the Garfield Ridge Trail. Soon you are climbing between low walls that keep you from walking on the delicate alpine vegetation. You'll see cushions of diapensia. Mountain sandwort blossoms white well into late summer, when the creeping mountain cranberry has formed red fruit in the rock crevices.

The trail rises more sharply toward the sky and the scattered crags of North Lafayette. The summit is only 0.25 mile plus a few yards from the Skookumchuck Trail. It's a beautiful place for lunch—on a good day; cold winds and cloud can buffet it and smother it.

If the day is one of unlimited visibility, your luck may also bring you the thrill of watching a sailplane glide silently over your aerie.

After that, your return is an anticlimax, although pleasant, down the same route you climbed.

25

Cannon Mountain

Distance (round trip): 7½ miles
Walking time: 6 hours
Vertical rise: 2,100 feet
Maps: USDA/FS 7½' Franconia; USGS 7½' Franconia

You can ride in a tramway cable car to the summit, so why climb Cannon Mountain on foot? Because only your two legs can make the mountain yours. Somehow this also improves the magnificent views of Franconia Notch and Mount Lafayette. For hikers aiming to climb all of New Hampshire's 4,000-footers, Cannon qualifies by 100 feet.

Skiers who have swooped down the snowy trails find that a summer climb, which pits them against this solid height unaided by tramway or T-bars, gives the mountain new meaning.

A rounded block seen from the notch, Cannon's stark cliffs loom before you as you drive north on the parkway. The mountain appears as a mass of stone on which evergreens cling with minimum success. Approach from the north, and you see its grassy ski slopes and trails like high pastures and giant paths down through the woods.

For a loop over the summit, climb the Kinsman Ridge Trail from the north and descend by the Hi-Cannon and Lonesome Lake Trails, returning through the notch to your car via the northern extension of the Pemi Trail.

Be forewarned that this is not a quiet, secluded hike. You'll be listening to the surf sound of traffic on the parkway and meeting tourists and campers.

HOW TO GET THERE

On I-93's Franconia Notch Parkway, take Exit 34B for the Cannon Mountain Tramway and Old Man Historic Site. Drive to the hikers' parking section of the tramway parking area.

N

0   0.5 mile

0   0.5 kilometer

Resort

BM

1965

Echo
Lake

93

Sewage Disposal

CANNON MOUNTAIN

WINTER SPORTS

AREA

SKI LIFT

SKI LIFT

SKI LIFT

AERIAL TRAMWAY

TRAIL

BM
1971

P

Eagle
Cliff

GREENLEAF

FRANCONIA   NOTCH   STATE   PARK

Profile
Lake

Old Man of the
Mountain

3566

3600

Cannon Mountain

RIDGE

LOOKOUT   TOWER

SKI LIFT

EST

KINSMAN

HIGH

CANNON

TRAIL

NOTCH

Bike Path

River

Pemi Tr

FRANCONIA

BRIDLE

Walker

LONESOME

Lafayette
Campground

BM 1770

Gravel
Pit

AROUND THE
LAKE TRAIL

onesome
Lake

LAKE

TR

ome Lake
Hut

CASCADE

BROOK

TR

Pemigewasset

FALLING

WATER

APT

2917

Dry

On Cannon Mountain

The asphalt covers a vanished field known as Profile Clearing. It was once the site of the immense Profile House described in Hike 19. As you leave your car, look up at the silhouette of the ridge south from the tramway. Perhaps you can discern a horizontal rock—the Cannon—aimed toward Mount Lafayette behind you and outlined against the sky. The Cannon can be seen more clearly from the Old Man of the Mountain Profile Plaza.

Before or after your hike, follow the signs to this memorial park on the shore of Profile Lake. On display is one of the four turnbuckles that for years gave the Old Man a facelift before this famous rock formation finally collapsed in May 2003. Seven steel rods, called "profilers," allow you to see where that profile stood out on the mountainside; when you line up your eyesight along them, there he is.

THE TRAIL

Your first trail for this loop hike, the Kinsman Ridge Trail, begins to the left of the tramway building, near the hikers' parking. A Kinsman Ridge Trail sign directs you onward along a service road to a clearing. Bear right. At the end of the clearing you'll see another Kinsman Ridge Trail sign on your left.

The trail climbs a steep bank, and at once you are on your way skyward. Steep for more than 1 mile, the trail gains altitude rapidly by a series of switchbacks. As you hike these switchbacks, you will notice wide openings in the trees above and below you, with great views of the notch. This is part of a glade ski trail, which also parallels the hiking trail a little farther up.

As the trail angles away from the tramway it becomes more difficult among rock slabs, which erosion has exposed. Watch your footing over roots and in gullies of rotten rock. Beyond this climb, the trail levels out on the east shoulder. After a passage through small spruce and fir, you come to a sharp right turn. A branch trail bears left to a breathtaking view from open ledges. North and south, the Franconia crests line the horizon: Eagle Cliff, Mount Lafayette, Mount Lincoln, Little Haystack, and Mount Liberty.

On a ridge several hundred yards north, and from a camouflage of evergreen scrub, the Cannon aims at Mount Lafayette. From this angle it appears in its true form—a balanced rock shelf.

Return to the main Kinsman Ridge Trail. Keep past the right turn leading back the way you came. The trail crosses the east shoulder, then dips into a wooded col. Soon you make a steep climb into the open again among rock slabs and alpine vegetation. All at once you hear voices and find yourself among people at the junction with the Rim Trail from the tramway. A large sign names the peaks in the panorama. From this junction, go left to the junction at which the Kinsman Ridge Trail begins to descend. Turn right onto a short trail to the summit. An observation tower puts you above the spruces. The tramway terminal extends out from a niche, where ski trails begin to dive down.

Joining tourists at the tower, you look down the notch and for an instant you are puzzled by a ribbon in the forest and toy cars. Across this highway, you see the Franconia Range, now part of a 360-degree view. Northward stretches the pastoral valley of the Gale River and Franconia village. South and west, a wilder panorama opens across Kinsman Mountain's two summits toward Mount Moosilauke.

When you're ready to descend, return to the Kinsman Ridge Trail. Follow it as it passes southward below the summit from the junction where you turned up to the tower. Follow it only about 0.5 mile to the Hi-Cannon Trail. The Kinsman Ridge Trail leaves right to continue its rugged way 15 miles to the southern end at the Lost River Road in Kinsman Notch. You take the Hi-Cannon Trail.

The Hi-Cannon Trail leads you past a lookoff ledge opening toward Kinsman Mountain on your right and Lonesome Lake below you. The trail swings through firs above cliffs, from which there are wide outlooks into the notch with its parallel ranges east and west. You climb down rocks on a ladder and pass the eave-like ledges called Cliff House on your left.

Continue down a rough stretch into less precipitous woods. Keep left past the Dodge Cutoff, which leads to Lonesome Lake. Hi-Cannon's switchbacks take you down to the Lonesome Lake Trail. Turn left and walk this graded path to the Lafayette Campground. Follow yellow blazes through the campground to a Pemi Trail sign, which faces away from you just before a footbridge.

Turn left on the Pemi Trail. It crosses the main entrance road before a bridge; look for the Pemi Trail sign. The Pemi Trail follows the stream, mostly on the route of the former Profile Lake Trail. Beavers have flooded the trail in several places, and you must hike around their ponds. Also, the trail is not well marked; at junctions, go right.

Instead of the Pemi Trail, you may prefer to walk the bike path from the Lafayette Campground. You'll find this path to the left of a log cabin across the bridge. Both routes take you to Profile Lake in about 2 miles. Here the Pemi Trail bears left along the west shore of the lake, whereas the bike path curves north under the parkway, then back toward the memorial park. Either way, you will be joining tourists and sightseers for the return to your car.

26

Kinsman Mountain

Distance (round trip): 10 miles

Walking time: 8 hours

Vertical rise: 3,400 feet

Maps: USDA/FS 7½' Sugar Hill; USGS 7½' Sugar Hill; USDA/FS 7½' Franconia; USGS 7½' Franconia; USDA/FS 7½' Lincoln; USGS 7½' Lincoln

Kinsman Mountain has two summits. A wooded col and 1 mile of the Kinsman Ridge Trail connect them. The mountain forms a divide that separates the Merrimack River tributaries from the Connecticut River watershed to the west.

The north peak, elevation 4,293 feet, drops away 500 feet to narrow Kinsman Pond and the roof of the shelter near the spruce-grown shore. Beyond, to the east, Lonesome Lake sparkles in the evergreen forest above Franconia Notch. Mount Lafayette, the giant of the region, rises across the notch.

The south peak's dome, elevation 4,358 feet, extends into the alpine-tundra zone above treeline due to topography and exposure and provides views in all directions. From both summits, the Franconia Range outlines the eastern horizon. Sun and clouds endlessly shift lighting effects across the slopes.

Although hikers most often climb Kinsman Mountain from Lonesome Lake, the route described here has the advantage of being less traveled and quite removed from the popularity of the Franconia Notch area. This hike takes you over both peaks and returns you by the same route. The Mount Kinsman Trail begins from the west in Easton, a township now grown back to woods from family farms of the 19th century. The Mount Kinsman Trail climbs to the Kinsman Ridge Trail, which traverses both summits.

Easton's settlement began at the conclusion of the Revolution. About 1783, Nathan Kinsman cut the first narrow woods track into the wilderness territory that is now Easton. He brought in tools and supplies on six

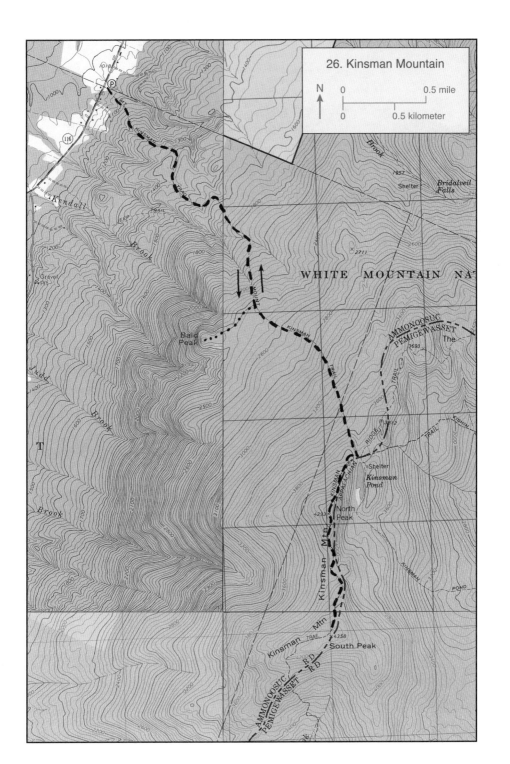

26. Kinsman Mountain

N

0   0.5 mile

0   0.5 kilometer

Kendall

Gravel
Pit

Bald
Peak

Judd

Brook

Brook

T

WHITE   MOUNTAIN   NA

Brook

Shelter

Bridalveil
Falls

1957

2711

2600

AMMONOOSUC
PEMIGEWASSET   The

3693

3612

3600

KUSHIN

TRAIL

KINSMAN   TRAIL

KINSMAN   TRAIL

RIDGE   TRAIL

APPALACHIAN

Shelter

Kinsman
Pond

KINSMAN

POND

North
Peak

4293

Kinsman   Mtn.

Kinsman   Mtn.   TRAIL

4358   South Peak

R.D
R.D

AMMONOOSUC
PEMIGEWASSET

116

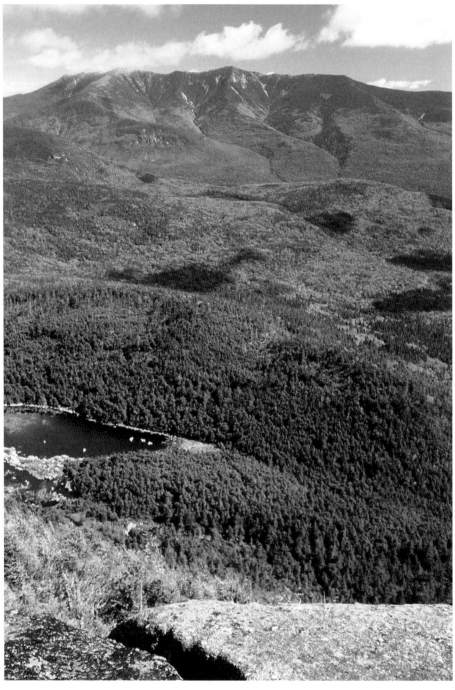

On North Kinsman

ROBERT J. KOZLOW

mules and built a log cabin on his grant of 600 acres. More settlers followed.

As in other mountain towns, the small meadows of Easton's valley and its rocky pastures fed and clothed an increasing population for 75 years until the Civil War. Then war casualties, hopes of easier western land, and cash wages from city industry drained away the young men. Now along NH 116, trees grow tall in the old farmland. The Mount Kinsman Trail crosses through some of this earlier farmland as it approaches the mountain's broad west slope.

HOW TO GET THERE

From NH 112 west of Kinsman Notch, take NH 116 and drive 6.4 miles to the new trailhead parking area for the Mount Kinsman Trail, on the right. Just ahead on the left can be seen a tennis court, and across the road is the Tamarack Tennis Camp.

From the village of Franconia, drive 4.6 miles south on NH 116. Look for the Tamarack Tennis Camp; the trailhead is 200 feet farther on the left.

THE TRAIL

After a 0.5-mile relocated section of the trail from the parking area, the trail joins the old route about 100 yards from an old sugar house.

Climbing more steeply, you approach a brook after 1.5 miles. Here once stood the Kinsman Cabin of the White Mountain National Forest, a fine example of axmanship. Cross the brook, bearing right, and climb up a steeper logging road. You will soon step over another brook with a mossy ledge on the left, then cross Flume Brook. A branch trail leads down to a ravine and cascade. Shortly beyond Flume Brook, the main trail turns sharply left. At 2.1 miles a branch trail to the right leads 0.25 mile to Bald Peak through woods to wide views from rocks amid blueberry bushes.

The main trail follows the dwindling brook.

You look up at the steep ridge ahead. The trail rises steadily through spruces and firs. Golden-crowned kinglets, feeding in the upper branches, give notice of their presence only by faint cheeping notes and by small flutterings. But if you look back on the steeper pitches, you can see the tiny birds in the treetops level with your eyes.

Among stunted evergreens, at 3.7 miles you reach the Kinsman Ridge Trail. (This trail is a long 16-mile trek over Cannon Mountain and Kinsman Mountain to Kinsman Notch.) Turn right, south, on the Kinsman Ridge Trail. Take note of this junction so that you'll recognize it on your return. The Kinsman Ridge Trail makes a narrow passage through evergreens and leads over rocky ledges to the north peak.

The north summit is partially wooded yet offers a sudden view of Mount Lafayette, which becomes breathtaking from the cliff reached by a short trail left, east, down among rocks and spruces. The jagged Franconia Range cuts across the eastern horizon.

To continue, climb back up the spur trail to the Kinsman Ridge Trail. Turn left and continue south. You descend to the col and climb up out of the evergreens to the bare south dome and the summit cairn. On several acres of open rock and dwarf spruces trimmed by the wind, you wander among abundant mountain plants, lichens, mosses, sedges, and grasses. In places, a matted turf has formed, held down by the roots of dwarf blueberry, Labrador tea, and mountain cranberry. Cool breezes and fine views make this the hike's ideal lunch setting.

In the afternoon, return north along the Kinsman Ridge Trail over the north peak. Watch for the left turn onto the Mount Kinsman Trail. Follow the route of your ascent, and remember not to be fooled at the corner where the Bald Peak spur trail invites you straight ahead; turn sharply right, down the straight logging road, then bear left across the brook.

27

Mount Moosilauke

Distance (round trip): 7½ miles

Walking time: 6 hours

Vertical rise: 2,500 feet

Maps: USDA/FS 7½' Mt. Kineo; USGS 7½' Mt. Kineo; USDA/FS 7½' Mt. Moosilauke; USGS 7½' Mt. Moosilauke

Rise early for Mount Moosilauke. It's a destination and an event. Bulking large on the southwestern border of the White Mountains, elevation 4,802 feet, the mountain stands massive and alone. Its bare summit commands wide views in a complete circle.

The Franconias, 14 miles northeast, march across the horizon. Far beyond them, Mount Washington appears with other Presidential peaks. More to the east, Mount Carrigain stands sentinel at the eastern approach to the Pemigewasset Wilderness, which is bordered on the south by Mounts Hancock, Osceola, Tripyramid, and the Sandwich Range. Directly south, smaller mountains scattered in the foothills blend toward isolated Mount Kearsarge—not to be confused with Mount Kearsarge North, Hike 41 in this book—and Mount Cardigan. Westward, across the verdant Connecticut River valley, Vermont's Green Mountains extend as far as Killington Peak, Mount Mansfield, and Jay Peak.

Mount Moosilauke has been popular for more than a hundred years. In 1860, Sam Holt built his stone Prospect House on the windswept summit. The opening ceremonies on the Fourth of July, according to one authority, attracted a thousand men and women. The gala crowd included a brass band, orators, militia, and Native Americans. Refreshments were served. The Carriage Road continued to bring guests from Warren.

The Carriage Road was still safe for horse-drawn rigs in 1917. Dartmouth College took over the hotel in 1920 and put in bunks and accommodations for 80 hikers. In the summer, students managed the Summit

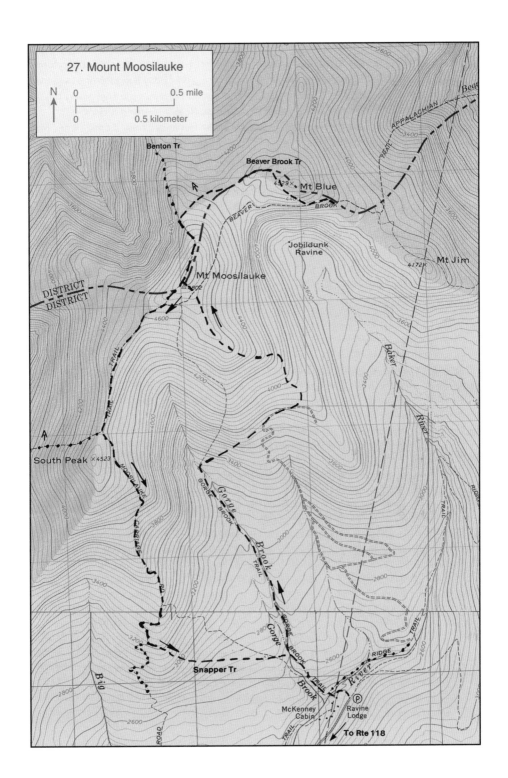

27. Mount Moosilauke

N   0   0.5 mile
     0   0.5 kilometer

Benton Tr

Beaver Brook Tr

Beaver

4529 × Mt Blue

BROOK

APPALACHIAN TRAIL

Beaver

Jobildunk
Ravine

Mt Jim

4172K

Mt Moosilauke

4802

DISTRICT
DISTRICT

Baker

River

TRAIL

South Peak × 4523

MOOSILAUKE

TRAIL

Gorge

GORGE BROOK

Brook

TRAIL

RIDGE

TRAIL

River

Snapper Tr

Gorge

GORGE BROOK

RIDGE TRAIL

Big

ROAD

Brook

TRAIL

McKenney
Cabin

Ravine
Lodge

P

To Rte 118

House, or Tip Top House as it was then called. Moosilauke has remained Dartmouth's mountain, although the Summit House burned in 1942. For a number of years the Dartmouth Outing Club maintained an emergency cabin below the summit, but by 1978 overuse and vandalism made its removal necessary. The college land is managed as a wilderness area, where overnight camping and open fires are not permitted. This policy of limited use is designed to protect the unique and fragile mountain environment. For more details, see the *Dartmouth Outing Guide* and www .dartmouth.edu/~doc/.

At all times the mountain can be cold and icy. Gales sweep down upon it with dangerous speed and intensity. Above treeline, clouds often shroud the rocks. The south shoulder, 1 mile long, is exposed to storms, and on a gloomy day suggests the beginning of the world despite the trail along the old Carriage Road traversing its length.

Note: Because of the damage from Tropical Storm Irene in 2011, there are plans to relocate Gorge Brook Trail along the brook.

HOW TO GET THERE

The trails starting near Dartmouth's Ravine Lodge offer the widest selection and most spectacular routes. In Warren, turn off NH 25 onto NH 118, and drive 5.9 miles to Ravine Road, the access road to the lodge. Turn left onto the road. If you are coming from the east, at the US 3 junction and traffic lights in North Woodstock, take NH 112 for

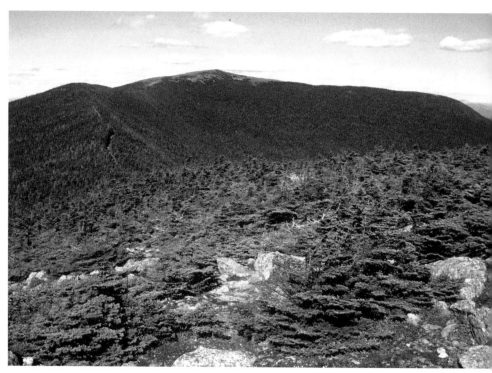

Mount Moosilauke

ROBERT J. KOZLOW

Franconia Notch Region

2.6 miles to NH 118. Continue 7.3 miles on NH 118 and turn right onto Ravine Road.

Drive 1.5 miles on Ravine Road to a turn-around. Head back along the road, and park on the right shoulder.

THE TRAIL

With adequate clothing for this above-tree-line climb and, of course, food and water, walk to the left side of the turnaround, north-west, near a sign for ALL TRAILS. Take the path down to the Baker River—here a large brook. Turn left, then in a few yards turn right over the footbridge. On the west bank, the Gorge Brook Trail begins to your left.

Take the path left along the bank. The trail swings right, and you begin the climb. After 0.6 mile the Snapper Trail branches left. (In combination with a section of the Moosilauke Carriage Road, it will be your return route.)

The Gorge Brook Trail rises steadily through mixed growths of hardwoods and spruces beside Gorge Brook's pools and cascades. A relocated section leads you about 0.5 mile to rejoin the trail. After the Ross McKenney Forest plaque, you are hiking on an earlier relocation; in 1990 Put Blodgett of the Dartmouth Outing Club completed this route to avoid the eroded and steeper former ascent.

At 2.3 miles you reach an outlook, with Mount Carr in the foreground, Mount Cardigan to the right, and Mount Kearsarge to the left. At 2.9 miles there are two views, the first eastward to the southern White Mountains, the second northeast over Jobildunc Ravine and Mounts Jim and Waternomee to Mount Lafayette and other White Mountain peaks.

The spruce/fir woods are the home of the 3,000-foot bird, the blackpoll warbler.

At about 3.1 miles the trail swings left at a rock staircase and begins what is called the "Balcony" section—a traverse across the east shoulder, with wide views southeast and southwest.

As you near treeline, a sign warns of the fragile alpine vegetation. Stay on the trail.

Scrubby heaths alternate with twisted evergreens. The trail, marked by cairns up the treeless ledges and alpine sward (look for mountain sandwort, three-leaved cinque-foil, and mountain cranberry vines), continues to the rocky summit, the rectangular stone foundations that once supported the Summit House, and the encompassing panorama.

For your descent, take the Moosilauke Carriage Road south along the rocky ridge. (If a storm threatens while you are on the summit, return by the Gorge Brook Trail.) The Dartmouth Outdoors Programs Office and the U.S. Forest Service have rebuilt the Carriage Road to limit erosion, provide emergency access, and make the trail more usable.

About 1 mile south of the summit on the Carriage Road, the Glencliff Trail, a link in the route the Appalachian Trail follows to Hanover and on into Vermont, drops down into the woods, right. A short way along the Glencliff Trail, a spur leads 0.2 mile west to the South Peak for a view of the forested Baker River Valley, Lake Tarleton, Mount Cube, Smarts Mountain, and various ponds.

Continue down the Carriage Road about 1.25 miles farther to the Snapper Trail, where you turn left. This former downhill racing ski trail is now a gentle grade. The loop is completed down at Gorge Brook Trail, about 1 mile.

28

Mount Garfield

Distance (round trip): 10 miles

Walking time: 8 hours

Vertical rise: 3,050 feet

Maps: USDA/FS 7½' Franconia; USGS 7½' Franconia; USDA/FS 7½' South Twin Mtn.; USGS 7½' South Twin Mtn.

Mount Garfield's rocky 4,500-foot summit commands a spectacular and unique view across a northern valley of the Pemigewasset Wilderness. Due south from Mount Garfield, Owl's Head—itself a 4,025-foot mountain—blocks the valley and forces Franconia Brook east, while forming a narrow gap below the Franconia Range. There, on the west, Mounts Lafayette and Lincoln rise to a heavy, peaked ridge. Mount Liberty stands alone, and Flume's spire farther south has its separate identity.

You look east down to the AMC's Garfield Ridge Campsite. Away off in that direction, Galehead Hut appears as a toy building among miles of evergreens. A line of summits shapes the eastern horizon and extends southward from North Twin over South Twin, Zealand Mountain, Guyot, and Bond to Bondcliff in the Pemigewasset River's East Branch valley.

The Garfield Trail approaches the mountain from US 3 and takes you up the long western slope to the steep cone.

HOW TO GET THERE

Drive north on I-93's Franconia Notch Parkway. Take Exit 35 onto US 3 and follow it about 4.8 miles. Watch for a hiker sign on your right. Turn right onto the forest service road. After you drive in you'll see a sign, FR 92. This is the Gale River Loop Road. Drive this very good road, with three new bridges, 1.2 miles to another bridge and parking on the right.

If you are coming from Twin Mountain, after you pass the Five Corners junction of

28. Mount Garfield

N

| 0 | 0.5 mile |
| 0 | 0.5 kilometer |

To Rt. 3

Trudeau Road with US 3, look for the hiker sign in 0.2 mile. Turn left onto FR 92.

THE TRAIL

The Garfield Trail is one of the pleasantest trails in the mountains. It begins at an embankment, keeps to a low ridge, and crosses Thompson Brook and Spruce Brook. At an intersection with a snowmobile trail with bridges spanning the brooks, use care to stay on the Garfield Trail uphill.

Your boots and legs find easy walking on this old tractor road that served the old summit fire tower. The grades are fine for steady walking. You continue past trees that form a protected corridor between areas logged in the early 1970s, now an interesting example of thickly sprouting growth after clear-cuts. Forest renewal can be compared because the trees along the trail grew after the forest fire of 1902. For years the trail traversed burned country. As often happens after forest fires, birches took over the scorched land. Their snowy trunks with the black splashes now shine in sunlight along your way.

After a short downhill grade below a ledgy bank, left, the trail climbs the steeper slope by long inclines between switchback turns. The birches yield to spruce/fir woods higher up. The trail steepens as it bears east. The evergreens become smaller, with gnarled birch and mountain ash interspersed beside the rocky outcrops and stone steps that now often form the trail.

Climbing around a corner to the right, you head south to join the Garfield Ridge Trail for the summit approach. (This trail comes up on the left from the Garfield Ridge Campsite.) The two trails ascend as one for a scramble of less than 0.25 mile up the final pitch. The trail suggests a crude rock stairway between low spruces, which offer handholds.

At the crest, turn left. It's 50 yards to the summit rocks and a former tower's concrete

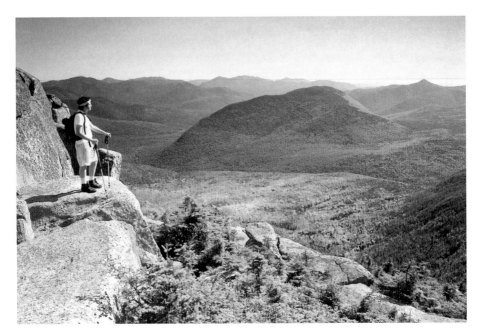

On Mount Garfield

foundation. (Garfield Ridge Trail continues to Mount Lafayette.)

In August 1907, Mount Garfield overlooked a holocaust. Twenty-five thousand acres, left in slash by the lumber king, J. E. "Ave" Henry, burst into flame as lightning struck the east side of Owl's Head. This fire was one of many that brought militant attention to the desolation caused by lumbermen and led to the Weeks Act of 1911 that established the White Mountain National Forest.

Old loggers, who chopped trees and earned a hard living in the forests they devastated, used to look back with nostalgia and tell yarns about J. E. Henry, who hired them and made a fortune. Henry, a once-barefoot poor boy, became legendary for his toughness, determination, and parsimony. The territory he clear-cut often went up in terrible forest fires.

There's no loop to this hike. Return by the same route you came.

29

Mount Osceola

Distance (Tripoli Road to main peak and return): 6½ miles

Walking time: 4½ hours

Vertical rise: 2,050 feet

Maps: USDA/FS 7½' Waterville Valley; USGS 7½' Waterville Valley; USDA/FS 7½' Mt. Osceola; USGS 7½' Mt. Osceola

Tripoli Road, Breadtray Ridge, Thornton Gap, Scar Ridge, Mad River—these colorful names from loggers' parlance enliven maps of the country that surrounds this peak named for the famous Seminole warrior. Mount Osceola dominates the upper end of Waterville Valley. Viewed from the west, its 4,340-foot elevation appears as a single summit, but seen from the east along the Kancamagus Highway, the East Peak's 4,156-foot shoulder enlarges the mountain.

HOW TO GET THERE

The most direct trail to the main summit begins at Waterville Valley's northwest pass, Thornton Gap. From Campton, drive east on NH 49, 10 miles up the Mad River. Turn left, and drive past the access road to Tecumseh Ski Area. This Tripoli Road crests 4.5 miles from NH 49 at the 2,300-foot pass. About 200 yards beyond, the Mount Osceola Trail enters the woods on the right (north), where there is a parking area.

If you are coming from Exit 31 off I-93, drive the Tripoli Road 7 miles to the parking area on the left.

THE TRAIL

At the start of the Mount Osceola Trail, you climb a stony section, but the grade is comfortable as the trail becomes a series of gravel switchbacks. More switchbacks take you up Breadtray Ridge. Most of the views along the way are overgrown, but there is a fine one of Mount Tecumseh's ski trails and Sandwich Mountain to the south beyond the green Waterville Valley. You cross a little brook on stepping stones. The trail swings right and left several times, and you walk through muddy patches, across moss-bordered ledges. Near the top of the ridge, the trail turns sharply right, east, and leads up to the level approach through summit spruces to the ledges and the sites of two former fire towers.

At the first site, where the older tower stood, take the path to the left for the view to the north. Then continue on to the site of the second tower and the extensive view from the ledges. Scrub spruce obscures some of the outlook.

You are now standing on the highest of the mountains encircling Waterville Valley, and the panorama off this isolated summit is vast. Slightly south of east, Mount Tripyramid's three peaks notch the horizon 5 miles away. An unusual nearby view extends north into the valley along Hancock Branch and the Kancamagus Highway. On the right of Mount Hancock, and more distant, Mount Carrigain's angular bulk gives you a line on Mount Washington, 22 miles away. Turning northwest, you can orient yourself by the sentinel, Mount Garfield, and find to your left Mounts Lafayette and Lincoln. Of the remaining Franconias, Mounts Liberty and Flume are pinnacles in the direction of Cannon Mountain. More to the west, Kinsman's north and south summits appear as a ridge, but Mount Moosilauke stands out as the important western peak.

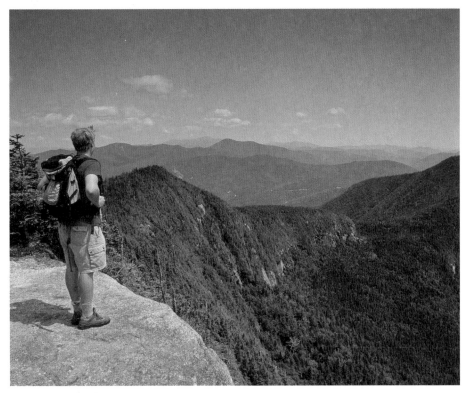

View from Mount Osceola

ROBERT J. KOZLOW

Return to the Tripoli Road by the route of ascent.

Those hardy souls who yearn to climb all the accepted 4,000-foot peaks will continue east on the Mount Osceola Trail and think nothing of the descent and climb to East Peak 1 mile away. They may even keep on down the steep and hazardous trail to Greeley Ponds and out to the Kancamagus Highway for a total of 7 miles from the Tripoli Road. (See Hike 7.) Or you may walk from Mad River Notch in the opposite direction past Greeley Ponds to Waterville Valley at Depot Camp. For either of these exploits, allow three hours more than for Osceola alone, and arrange for transportation at the end.

30

Mount Tripyramid

Distance (round trip): 11 miles

Walking time: 7 hours

Vertical rise (including all three peaks): 3,000 feet

Maps: USDA/FS 7½' Mt. Tripyramid; USGS 15' Mt. Chocorua; USDA/FS 7½' Waterville Valley; USGS 7½' Waterville Valley

The name describes the three peaks; it says nothing about the two slides. For pure joy in climbing, the North Slide is hard to beat. You choose your own way over the angular ledges. There is little danger in dry weather. A wild and extensive view opens behind you.

From the Livermore Road out of Waterville Valley, you hike a loop up the exciting North Slide, over the three peaks, down the treacherous South Slide, and back to the road. The slides tore out the woods and rocks on both North and South Peaks in 1885. The slides are completely unlike, the North Slide being ledges, the South Slide rocks and gravel. The three peaks rise in a line from a ridge about 1 mile long. North Peak's elevation is 4,180 feet. Middle Peak reaches to 4,140 feet. South Peak crests at 4,100 feet.

HOW TO GET THERE

From Campton, drive east on NH 49, 10 miles up the Mad River. Turn left onto the Tripoli Road and drive past the access road to Tecumseh Ski Area. At 1.8 miles from NH 49, turn right across the Mad River's West Branch. Just beyond the bridge, turn sharply left at a gate into the parking area. The road to the right continues on to Waterville village.

THE TRAIL

The hike begins at a kiosk at the east end of the parking area. Turn onto the Livermore Road. This shaded gravel road is also the Livermore Trail. Keep past the Greeley Ponds Trail on your left. You soon cross a bridge over the Mad River.

30. Mount Tripyramid

N

| 0 | 0.5 mile |
| 0 | 0.5 kilometer |

You'll pass other trails that are part of the hiking and ski touring system maintained by the Waterville Valley Athletic and Improvement Association. At 2.1 miles Cascade Path bears right across Avalanche Brook on a creosoted, heavy-timbered bridge. Don't take it. Stay on your side of the brook, the north or left bank, on the Livermore Road.

This will bring you to the trail on the right for Tripyramid's South Slide at 2.6 miles. It is your return route after you climb over the mountain's three summits. Another 0.5 mile and you pass through the opening that was once Avalanche Camp back during the ax/crosscut-saw era in the White Mountains. You are approaching the start of the climb. Watch for a hairpin turn to the left at 3.6 miles. The Mount Tripyramid Trail to the North Slide drops off the road to your right at the corner. (The Livermore Road continues and becomes a hikers' trail over Livermore Pass and down to the Kancamagus Highway 4 miles north.)

Note: The Slide is dangerous when wet or icy. For a trail that bypasses it, proceed up the Livermore Road 0.25 mile and turn right onto the Scaur Ridge Trail. This trail loops eastward toward Scaur Peak and a

Mount Tripyramid   ROBERT J. KOZLOW

ridge connecting with North Tripyramid, where it joins the Pine Bend Brook Trail coming up from the Kancamagus Highway to the North Peak. This safer route is only about 0.75 mile longer than the North Slide.

On a dry, warm day, climb down from the hairpin turn, and cross Avalanche Brook. Climb the bank beyond the brook, and follow the trail upstream, left, for a 0.5-mile walk on this former logging road to the base of the slide.

The yellow blazes on the rocks are faded and difficult to see. Take time to look for them—and to turn and admire the view behind you. If you wander off, just remember to bear right near the top. You'll see two large cairns there. The trail enters the spruces at the upper left corner.

The short remaining climb in the woods takes you to the North Peak. The tremendous 180-degree view is now overgrown, but look for glimpses of the Franconia Range and Mount Washington—all from a rare angle across the Kancamagus Highway and over the forests of the Pemigewasset Wilderness.

The Pine Bend Brook Trail joins the Mount Tripyramid Trail to become the route south down the ridge. The Pine Bend Brook Trail ends after 0.5 mile at the Sabbaday Brook Trail, left (from the Kancamagus Highway). You keep straight along and begin the climb up Middle Peak. There's a good view west from a ledge near the summit of Middle Peak. Continue on to South Peak.

Descending, you come to the South Slide and to forested vistas stretching away west. The two Flat Mountain Ponds lie in a hollow left of Sandwich Mountain. Ski trails identify Mount Tecumseh. Mount Moosilauke dominates the western horizon.

About 60 yards down the slide, the Kate Sleeper Trail comes in on your left from Mount Whiteface. Keep going down the slide. Watch for rolling gravel and loose rocks as you place your feet. At the base of the slide, bear right. The trail enters the woods, crosses several small brooks, then makes a crossing over Avalanche Brook to the terminus at Livermore Road. Turn left down the road for the 2.6-mile return to your car.

31

Between the Notches: Zeacliff

Distance (round trip via Twinway): 8 miles; (round trip, including loop through Zealand Notch): 9¾ miles

Walking time (via Twinway): 5 hours; (through Zealand Notch): 7 hours

Vertical rise: 1,500 feet

Maps: USDA/FS 7½' Crawford Notch; USGS 7½' Crawford Notch

The roadless upper watershed of the Pemigewasset River's East Branch separates Franconia Notch and Crawford Notch and their adjacent mountains. Part of this is now the Pemigewasset Wilderness. Long known as the "Pemi Wilderness," it has become an officially designated Wilderness by act of Congress. The main highways circle this country and leave the tourist unaware of the forested valleys and peaks between the two sections of the White Mountains. A hike to Zeacliff fills this vacancy.

You approach this great outlook (elevation 3,600 feet) along an abandoned railroad grade once used to haul logs out to the mills. The grade parallels the Zealand River toward its source. Beavers dam the branching streams. Zealand Pond, at the end of swampy meadows, has two outlets. Mid-June is a fine time to walk the Zealand Trail and look for birds. At that time, too, the rhodora blooms pink across the bogs.

Perched above the pond, the AMC's Zealand Falls Hut offers accommodations to 36 hikers and a view directly to Mount Carrigain.

Zeacliff is about 1.5 miles above the hut and is reached by the Twinway, a mountain trail. This steady climb brings you to Zeacliff's lookoff ledge above wooded valleys and mountains stretching away south and east, with views of Zealand Notch and Whitewall Mountain, both seared by fire during and after the logging days of the 1880s and early 1900s. This old slashed and burned country has grown up largely to hardwoods. Former logging roads appear as green ribbons along distant contours of lighter growth. Sometimes ravens hover over the cliffs.

HOW TO GET THERE

To reach the beginning of the Zealand Trail and the railroad grade, drive to the Zealand Campground on US 302, 2.5 miles east from Twin Mountain village. Turn south on the forest service's Zealand Road, which crosses the Ammonoosuc River and leads up a steep hill to a steadily ascending valley. Pass the Sugarloaf Camping Areas, and continue to the Zealand Road's end, 3.5 miles from the highway.

THE TRAIL

Walk to the south end of the parking area. The Zealand Trail follows the railroad grade except for short sections cut through the woods where the railroad once crossed the Zealand River for short distances. In this way the trail keeps west of the dwindling river, which divides into its source streams. You approach Zealand Pond through a boggy country of meadows and beaver ponds.

This open country has varying water levels due to the beavers' instinct to dam all running water. You'll find that most of the brooks have footbridges and that the wooden walkways help keep your feet dry. The plants and birds in this habitat include the tiny insectivorous sundew clinging to a rotten log half-submerged in water. High on a dead stub, the sturdy olive-sided flycatcher calls out stridently *hic-three-beers*. During May the shadbushes, one species of which can grow to 20 feet, bloom in white splendor. Sections of the old railroad grade are visible above the bogs.

At 2.3 miles from the start of the Zealand Trail, the A-Z Trail enters from the left. (The A-Z Trail connects to trails from the Crawford Depot area and Crawford Notch's Willey

31. Between the Notches: Zeacliff

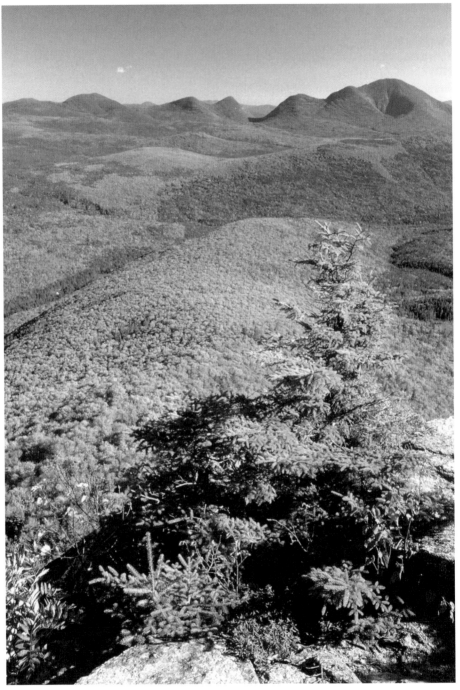

Zeacliff in the fall

ROBERT J. KOZLOW

Range.) You cross the north outlet of Zealand Pond and follow the east shore. At the south end, where you make a sharp right turn, the Ethan Pond Trail enters from the left. (The Ethan Pond Trail leads through Zealand Notch.) Keep right on the Twinway Trail, across a wet section at the south outlet of Zealand Pond. Soon you climb the steep rise to the Zealand Falls Hut, 2,700 feet elevation. (The AMC keeps the hut open in winter on a self-service basis. Cross-country skiing on plenty of good snow makes this region of special interest.)

Behind the hut, take the Twinway Trail up past the Lend-a-Hand Trail at the right. (The Lend-a-Hand Trail climbs Mount Hale.) Cross the small Whitewall Brook above the falls. The Twinway Trail is rough and steep compared to the previous railroad grade. White birches grow smaller as the trail climbs into stunted spruces. It emerges on the rocky summit of the ridge leading toward Zealand Mountain, Mount Guyot, and South Twin. At a VIEW sign just before the summit rocks, bear left for the top of Zeacliff, which is on a short loop off the Twinway Trail. The cliff overlooks Zealand Notch and faces Whitewall Mountain.

You are looking across the eastern area of the Pemigewasset Wilderness and the Lincoln Woods Scenic Area, thousands of acres preserved in their wildness. Mount Carrigain towers over the forest, a spruce-clad pyramid topped by an observation platform. Ponds draining into the Pemigewasset River's East Branch glisten in the valleys. To the left of Carrigain you sight through Carri-

gain Notch next to Mount Lowell. To the right of Carrigain, Mount Hancock is a solid outline. Closer and to the west, Mount Bond reaches away south from its barren crown.

If you are in shape for a tough and dramatic descent, your return need not be back to the hut the way you came. Fair warning: This loop is not for picnickers. If you decide you're rugged enough, walk west along the Twinway almost 0.25 mile, and turn left onto the Zeacliff Trail. It at once drops off the side of the mountain into evergreen forest with eroded roots, rocks, and bare rock faces sometimes more than 10 feet high. You descend into a forest of white birches along a southerly ridge, then drop again in a series of steep pitches between level little plateaus. Through the leaves you may catch glimpses of the slides and cliffs of Whitewall Mountain across Zealand Notch.

You reach the bottom of the ridge at a stretch of spruce and balsam woods before you come to the alders along Whitewall Brook. It's a tidy little stream, and you can cross on rocks, usually. Beyond it you climb a wooded slide into the open of barren rock slabs and jagged talus. The formations suggest an abandoned quarry. Follow blue blazes up the rock-scramble to the Ethan Pond Trail. Turn left, north, for the hike back to Zealand Pond along the old railroad grade. This loop covers a distance of 3 miles, as compared to the 1.5 miles back the way you came from Zealand Falls Hut. But it's an experience to pass through Zealand Notch before hiking out to your car.

Mount Washington Region

And that night in the log cave, on the fragrant boughs, I listened to the wind outside
and I was snug in a mountain fastness and
knew the feeling that went with the strange
word: fastness. Peaks out there in the darkness. Mount Washington, Jefferson, Adams,
Madison.

–Daniel Doan,
Our Last Backpack

32

Pinkham Notch: The Crew-Cut Trail

Distance (round trip): 2¼ miles

Walking time: 1¼ hours

Vertical rise: 400 feet

Maps: USDA/FS 7½' Mt. Washington SE; USGS 7½' x 15' Mt. Washington; USDA/FS 7½' Carter Dome; USGS 7½' Carter Dome

Pinkham Notch appears less spectacular near the highway than either Franconia or Crawford Notch. But situated close under Mount Washington's eastern ravines, Pinkham Notch has its own distinction: it's a climbing center. It's as near as you can drive on a main highway (NH 16) to the most impressive mountain in New England—Mount Washington. Major trails pass through or start in Pinkham Notch. It's the mountain climbers' base, a takeoff for the Presidential Range.

Pinkham Notch has changed since 1826, when Daniel Pinkham built the road through his grant between Jackson and Randolph. Now there's the wide highway. Traffic on NH 16 would astound Daniel Pinkham. The AMC's Pinkham Notch Visitor Center, established in 1920, has outgrown the original log cabins. This modern headquarters for the AMC's Hut and Trail System has become a complex of buildings, with accommodations for more than 100 guests at the Joe Dodge Lodge.

An introductory hike, the Crew-Cut Trail winds through hardwood forest to the reward of a lookout ledge at the north end of Pinkham Notch.

HOW TO GET THERE

The AMC's Pinkham Notch Visitor Center is west off NH 16, about 11 miles north of the junction of NH 16 and US 302 in Glen and about 10.5 miles south of the junction of NH 16 and US 2 in Gorham. The parking lot is big, but it may be crowded.

32. Pinkham Notch: The Crew-Cut Trail

THE TRAIL

The Tuckerman Ravine Trail begins behind the Pinkham Notch Visitor Center Trading Post. About 150 feet along it, watch for the sign to the Old Jackson Road, which is part of the Appalachian Trail and thus has white blazes. Bear right on this trail. Cross a work road, following the white blazes. The trail leads you through the woods 0.3 mile to a junction where the Blanchard Loop and Connie's Way ski trails cross it. Continue on the Old Jackson Road, which is soon crossed by another cross-country ski trail, the Link Ski Trail. Blue diamonds mark these ski trails.

Ahead on the Old Jackson Road you'll see a wooden bridge. Immediately after the bridge, the Crew-Cut Trail branches right.

Follow the blue blazes across a seasonal brook and another brook, through beech and yellow birch trees. Across a third brook, keep straight past the George's Gorge Trail, left. Continue following the blue blazes. The trail climbs over a knoll and enters an area of broken ledges under the tall trees as it approaches the base of a cliff. At 0.5 mile from the Old Jackson Road, you come to a junction with Liebeskind's Loop.

Ignore the mileage for Lila's Ledge on the trail sign. It's actually intended for Brad's Bluff, so it is incorrect. Turn left and take Liebeskind's Loop 0.1 mile to the spur trail on the right. Follow the spur trail 0.1 mile to the lookout called Lila's Ledge. This pinnacle offers a wide view of the Wildcat Ski Area, Pinkham Notch, and up to Mount Washington.

Return to your car by the same route you came.

33

Low's Bald Spot

Distance (round trip): 4¼ miles

Walking time: 2¾ hours

Vertical rise: 1,050 feet

Maps: USDA/FS 7½' Mt. Washington SE; USGS 7½' x 15' Mt. Washington

The half-day excursion from Pinkham Notch to Low's Bald Spot takes you to a 3,000-foot opening on Mount Washington's eastern slope. By easy trails you experience the mountain's sweep and primitive power. You look away to the peaks north and west. Wide views open east to the Carter Range and south through Pinkham Notch. Low's Bald Spot gives you mountain air and sunlight, distant skies, and the near scent of fir balsam.

HOW TO GET THERE

Turn off NH 16 for parking at the AMC's Pinkham Notch Visitor Center. The center is about 11 miles north of the junction of NH 16 and US 302 in Glen and about 10.5 miles south of the junction of NH 16 and US 2 in Gorham.

THE TRAIL

Behind the Pinkham Notch Visitor Center Trading Post, take the Tuckerman Ravine Trail for about 150 feet to the sign for the Old Jackson Road on your right. White-blazed, the Old Jackson Road is part of the Appalachian Trail. It was once a route for horse-drawn vehicles from Pinkham Notch to the carriage road, now the auto road. Follow the white blazes straight across a junction with the Blanchard and Connie's Way ski trails at about 0.3 mile, and again across the Link Ski Trail. Blue diamonds mark these ski trails. You cross a wooden bridge. Here the Crew-Cut Trail branches right. Keep straight up the hill ahead. After crossing a brook, you see George's Gorge Trail come in on your right at about 1 mile.

trail levels somewhat, passing the Raymond Path at 1.7 miles, to your left, and then the Nelson Crag Trail, also left. (See Hike 37, The Alpine Garden.) By now, you'll be hearing vehicles on the auto road. Climb onward over rocks and through an old gravel pit. You come out on the auto road above the 2-mile marker.

On the other side of the road, take the Madison Gulf Trail. You are continuing on the Appalachian Trail as it enters the Great Gulf Wilderness.

Follow the Madison Gulf Trail 0.25 mile to a branch trail, right, and the short climb to Low's Bald Spot. (The Madison Gulf Trail continues to the Great Gulf, up to treeline, and to the AMC's Madison Spring Hut in the barren col between Mount Adams and Mount Madison, the northeastern pinnacle of the Presidential Range. The trail is also a link to the Great Gulf Trail and the trails leaving the Gulf for the high peaks. The entire Madison Gulf Trail takes 5 hours of steady hiking and strenuous climbing up the steep headwall of Madison Gulf.)

After the short climb from the main trail, you cross two ledges before getting to the highest, Low's Bald Spot. Look north across the lower valley of the Great Gulf and the West Branch of the Peabody River to Mount Adams and Mount Madison. Far to the northeast is the Mahoosuc Range. On the east you see Wildcat Mountain, the Carters, and Imp Face. West is the headwall of Huntington Ravine topped by Nelson Crag and the bare cone of Mount Washington, a desert of jumbled stones rising in unforgettable contrast to the green trees below. Up there, earth's verdure emerges miraculously from its mineral source. Yet the grim environment might suggest to you an atomic blast's rubble. If it does, you are happy to hear the birds singing in the nearby spruces and to see hikers on the trails, and almost relieved to hear autos grinding up the road.

Continue on the Old Jackson Road. It crosses several brooks and rises about 600 feet before you make a sharp left turn onto a 1977 trail cut to avoid a section of the auto road. Climb the steep rock steps here. The

34

Glen Boulder

Distance (to Glen Boulder and back):
3¼ miles

Walking time: 3½ hours

Vertical rise: 1,750 feet

Maps: USDA/FS 7½' Stairs Mtn.; USGS
7½' Stairs Mtn.

West of the highway (NH 16) through Pinkham Notch and about 8 miles north of Jackson, a high bare ridge supports Glen Boulder among lesser rocks. Outlined against the sky, the great boulder appears about to topple into the notch.

A climb to this landmark also lifts you rapidly to treeline, with its strange ecology of ledge and lichen. Glen Boulder is a good destination for an afternoon. Besides being the shortest route to treeline on this eastern side of Mount Washington, it tests your legs and offers a superb panorama of mountainous slopes, valleys, and summits.

HOW TO GET THERE

The Glen Boulder Trail, cut and marked in 1905, leaves the parking circle and restrooms at Glen Ellis Falls on the west side of NH 16, 9 miles north of Jackson. (Glen Ellis Falls, reached by a tunnel under the highway and by stone steps into a ravine, sluices spectacularly from a ledge 70 feet into a rocky pool. The water of the Ellis River pours out as from a pitcher. Mist cools the air blowing across the evergreens and the pool.)

THE TRAIL

The Glen Boulder Trail, blazed yellow, rises from the parking area's south corner and swings right, climbing to level woods. Here you pass through a typical 2,000-foot-elevation hardwood forest. Big yellow birches, beeches, and other deciduous trees shade striped maples, hobblebushes, and ferns. Wood thrushes and hermit thrushes inhabit the ground and undergrowth.

A second steep pitch takes you to the base of a cliff. Just above the cliff the trail reaches a junction, on your right, with the Direttissima, a trail leading 1 mile to the Pinkham Notch Visitor Center.

Climbing on, the Glen Boulder Trail swings left and soon begins a steep ascent. At 0.8 mile, you cross a ski-touring trail marked with blue squares. After steady climbing, you next cross a brook and approach the

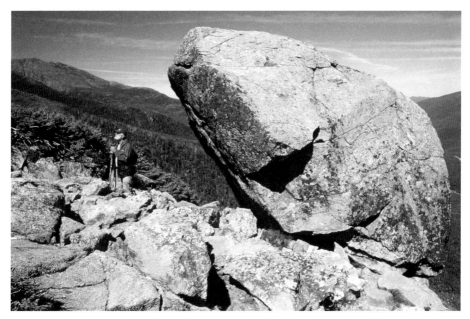

Glen Boulder

abruptly rising shoulder. From here you climb from treeline through alpine vegetation, wind-and-snow-flattened black spruce/balsam—known as krummholz—over steep ledges and rocks, for 0.25 mile up to Glen Boulder.

Facing south, you look away 20 miles to Mount Chocorua's rocky tower. The sweep is to your left over the Saco River and Ellis River valleys to nearby Wildcat Ridge and around over Pinkham Notch to Mount Washington.

The Glen Boulder Trail continues steeply above treeline and through scrub spruce for more than 1.5 miles to the Davis Path. This fine route to Mount Washington should be undertaken only by seasoned climbers. From Glen Boulder to Mount Washington's summit via the Davis Path and the Crawford Path is a rugged, long 4 miles. A loop to the AMC's Lakes of the Clouds Hut adds another mile. These trails are more difficult than they appear and take longer than you might estimate; allow at least three hours of constant walking and climbing, even in good weather. If there's any sign of clouds descending, rain, or storm, turn around at the boulder and descend to your car.

This is also a warning to the beginner and to the exhilarated devotee who feels a powerful urge to go on just a while longer. You planned a short climb to Glen Boulder. Enjoy yourself there, and then head back.

And don't take the Direttissima, or you'll end up at the Pinkham Notch Visitor Center. Keep to the right at that junction.

35

Tuckerman Ravine

Distance (to the Snow Arch and back):
6¼ miles

Walking time: 5¾ hours

Vertical rise: 2,500 feet

Maps: USDA/FS 7½' Mt. Washington
SE; USGS 7½' x 15' Mt. Washington

A glacial cirque of rocks and cliffs gouged at treeline by prehistoric ice, this dramatic basin in Mount Washington's southeast slope can be an exciting destination as well as the beginning of the strenuous upper climb to the summit. Open-front shelters amid spruces surround little Hermit Lake. The headwall's precipices are famous for spring skiing when they are banked by tremendous snow accumulations; they drip veils of water that gather at the base to undercut the remaining snow and form the Snow Arch, which survives well into summer.

On the north, the cliff named Lion Head juts into the ravine toward the south wall, which is crowned by Boott Spur. East, from the open half-basin, the view extends across Pinkham Notch to Wildcat Ridge and the Carter Range. Climbing directly from the notch into this giant amphitheater, the Tuckerman Ravine Trail follows a graded tractor path up to Hermit Lake and the shelters and then becomes the popular path up to the Snow Arch.

HOW TO GET THERE

The AMC's Pinkham Notch Visitor Center is west off NH 16, about 11 miles north of the junction of NH 16 and US 302 in Glen and about 10.5 miles south of the junction of NH 16 and US 2 in Gorham. Turn in and park in the long parking strip, where other hikers, young and old, are preparing to leave for the trails or are returning. Here at the visitor center you'll find information on the trails, a snack bar, and other facilities. (Here also you may buy the permit required if you plan to

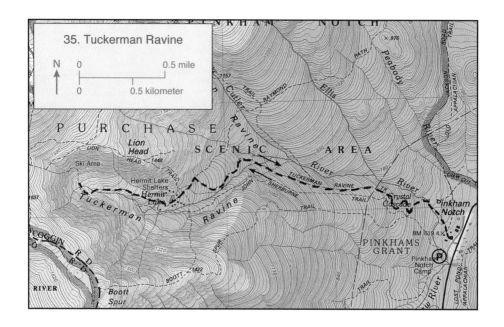

35. Tuckerman Ravine

N 0 ———————— 0.5 mile

0 ———————— 0.5 kilometer

stay overnight in the ravine's Hermit Lake shelters.)

THE TRAIL

To reach the Tuckerman Ravine Trail, walk behind the visitor center's Trading Post. Hikers intending to climb above treeline should take to heart the warning sign about adequate clothing and food and good physical condition. The wide tractor path presents equable grades, but on the upper section leading to the ravine, eroded stones require careful stepping, and it's all uphill. (The descent can be even more taxing on middle-aged knees.)

The path crosses the Cutler River, named soon after the Revolution for an explorer, the Reverend Manasseh Cutler. His party changed the mountain's name from Agiochook to Washington. Beyond the footbridge over this stream whose source is far up under the headwall, you turn a right corner and begin to climb. Soon, on the right again, take a few steps up to a ledge across from

Crystal Cascade, one of the most impressive in the mountains.

The path continues to climb by easy switchbacks through a forest of big yellow birch and beech. These woods are favored by the winter wren—in summer only, despite his name. He's notable for his small size and for his vertical tail feathers. You hear his voluble song more often than you see him in the underbrush.

After about 1 mile, the woods change to spruce and fir interspersed with white birch and mountain ash. You may expect to catch glimpses of boreal chickadees in the evergreens. Their brown caps differentiate them from the common black-capped chickadees. The boreals sing a husky series of notes lacking one or two "dees." Once rare, they seem to have discovered and taken over the cool White Mountains, which lie south of their regular habitat.

Continue past the Huntington Ravine Trail, which branches right. Cross a wooden

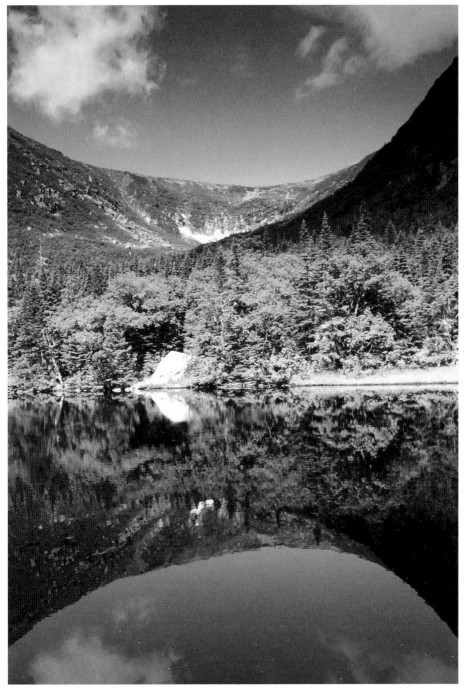

Hermit Lake and Tuckerman Ravine

bridge over the Cutler River, where hikers often rest and admire the view toward Wildcat Ridge.

Two miles of steady climbing take you past the Raymond Path on the right and around a wide S-turn into the ravine. You pass the Lion Head Trail, right, and the Boott Spur Link on the left. The ravine opens up to the wide sky and bare rocks. At 2.4 miles the shelters appear on side trails and across Hermit Lake.

The central building, known as "Howard Johnson's" or "HoJo's," burned in 1972 but has been rebuilt and serves as an information center and caretaker's lodge. No meals are available. The name, applied satirically years ago to an earlier building that also burned, expressed the attitude of various salty characters who preferred the primitive ravine when it had only two log shelters. Cliffs tower above, and to the west, beyond a rocky slope edged with scrub spruce, the headwall rises perpendicularly toward the clouds that coast steadily eastward.

The shelters and tent platforms are for hikers who purchase permits at the Pinkham Notch Visitor Center. Overuse of the limited area, as throughout the mountains at certain popular spots, made regulations necessary. Camping in the woods was discontinued to preserve the delicate subalpine soil, trees, and plant life. Hikers should bring their own lunches and carry out their trash. If cooking is planned, they should carry portable stoves; wood or charcoal fires are not allowed. The endangered ecology is responding to these conservation measures. Hikers realize the problem and are helping.

The trail will now lead you to the headwall and the Snow Arch. (This is still Tuckerman Ravine Trail, continuing from the shelter areas on the north, or right, side of the brook.) It finds a route at the base of the cliffs and circles the headwall to the north of the cliffs. Be careful. Pay attention to your footing. On holiday weekends, hikers form a moving line of figures on the trail up and across the headwall. Balmy weather in the ravine sometimes changes to icy wind and clouds above; plan on its doing so.

Never walk under the Snow Arch. Huge chunks fall off without warning. By late summer it has melted away into the Cutler River.

The summit of Mount Washington is only 1 mile from the Snow Arch, but it's a mile to remember. Time is a better measure: it will take two hours if you are accustomed to scrambling over rocks at such an angle. The 1,000 feet of elevation gain to the summit from the diverging trails above the headwall (known as Tuckerman Junction) appears to be less because above treeline there is no familiar sight for estimating distance. The landscape is as strange as the sudden storms are fierce. And the higher you climb, the fiercer they get; the protection of the ravine is often welcome.

36

Mount Washington

Distance (round trip): 9¼ miles
Walking time: 9 hours
Vertical rise: 3,800 feet
Maps: USDA/FS 7½' Mt. Washington SE; USGS 7½' x 15' Mt. Washington

By its western approach, the route of this climb to the 6,288-foot summit of Mount Washington takes you up the steep and scenic Ammonoosuc Ravine from near the Mount Washington Cog Railway's base station. Just above treeline, the AMC's Lakes of the Clouds Hut offers shelter if the weather turns frigid and stormy. Mount Washington's rocky cone and the summit buildings are 1,200 feet higher and 1.5 miles away at the top of the trail laid out by the legendary mountaineer, Ethan Allen Crawford.

On the summit, you'll meet tourists who came on the cog railway or in their cars. They think you are out of your mind for climbing when you could ride. For the dyed-in-the-wool hiker, once or twice on the summit is enough, unforgettable as it is.

When planning the hike, check the Mount Washington Observatory's summit forecasts at www.mountwashington.org.

Save this climb for a day of matchless clarity, so rare on this peak of cloud, rain, and storm. Waiting for a clear day will prove worthwhile. Then the far horizon will be the limit of vision, and you'll see a great sweep of country that includes most of New Hampshire and parts of Maine, Vermont, and the Province of Quebec. You will stand at the center of a circle 200 miles in diameter, enclosing hundreds of mountains and valleys in 30,000 square miles. Perhaps you'll see the ocean to the east, blending with the sky.

HOW TO GET THERE

Leave US 302 at Fabyan and drive on the Base Road 5.5 miles to hiker parking on the

36. Mount Washington

right. You are 0.25 mile west of the base station.

THE TRAIL

The Ammonoosuc Ravine Trail starts at the east side of the large parking area. Shoulder your pack. It should contain a heavy sweater, thick wool shirt or insulated jacket, and a parka, warm cap, and gloves. Rain gear is good insurance. Your lunch and water should be supplemented by emergency food for two meals. If you climb in shorts, carry warm pants. You are heading for an arctic-alpine zone.

This parking area in the woods restricts the views that were so impressive as you approached the former trailhead at the base station. From there, the barren heights rise to desolate rocks and make you acutely aware of the rugged ascent. At the relocated start in the woods you are less likely to evaluate your fitness realistically. Also missing is the busy scene around the station, where gala-clad vacationers watch engineers in overalls and grimy firemen and brakemen or visit the gift shop and snack bar while awaiting train time. Engines with tilted boilers puff smoke and steam from coal fires and push passenger cars up the steep track by means of a drive gear engaging the steel pins set between the two walls of a center rail. This was the invention of New Hampshire–born Sylvester March. In 1869 President Ulysses S. Grant rode up the mountain on the first train, along with P. T. Barnum. Grant spent the night down at the Crawford House, but evidently Barnum spent the night on the summit, in either the Summit House or the Tip Top House, because he declared that the next morning's sunrise was the "second greatest show on earth." (No overnight accommodations now.)

The Ammonoosuc Ravine Trail leads up an easy slope from the parking area into a forest of spruce, fir, and birch. Franklin Brook is a stone-to-stone crossing. Beyond this gully are two old water pipes leading to the base station. Then the trail swings southeast away from the sound of steam engines and descends to its former route, about 1 mile from your car. Keep to the right up this old path beside the Ammonoosuc River. In the next mile you pass a tributary brook and continue to Gem Pool below a fine waterfall.

Across the stream you begin the precipitous ascent up steps among spruces. The trail faces you like a rough, rocky wall of earth reinforced with tree roots. Partway up this first steep section, at 2.3 miles, a small sign and a spur trail on the right offer you the opportunity to see the brook's glittering torrent pour down a long stone sluice formed by ledges. Climbing on up the main trail, you pass wide carpets of green-leaved wood sorrel, which blooms white in mid-July. You come to another high falls, where at this altitude the mountain or alpine avens blooms yellow in early July. Among open rocks, Labrador tea puts out white frilly flowers, and bog laurel shows pink blooms above moist turf.

Ten minutes' climbing brings you to another falls and brook crossing, then soon to another. The spruces dwindle to the ancient dwarf clumps twisted and flattened by winds at treeline. The scrub growth ends at the vast expanse of rocks, which extends to Mount Washington's summit on your left. Follow cairns and blue paint blazes the last 100 yards over the ledges to the Lakes of the Clouds Hut on the windswept col between Mount Washington and Mount Monroe on your right.

This AMC hut is the highest in the hut system. Stone walls first withstood the gales at 5,012 feet in 1915. Now expanded and modernized, the hut is a popular stopover. Many hikers cross from the Tuckerman

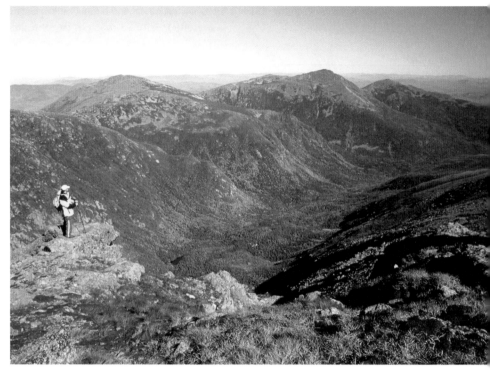

Gulfside Trail

ROBERT J. KOZLOW

Ravine Trail, descend from Mount Washington, or traverse the 7-mile ridge from Crawford Notch. The hut is the terminus of the Ammonoosuc Ravine Trail.

Here the wind, and often clouds in the form of dense fog, as well as violent summer storms of rain, lightning, and sleet, decide for you whether or not you climb on toward the summit on this try. You will probably understand why unwary hikers above treeline on Mount Washington have perished from exposure in the summer.

When the weather is favorable, take the Crawford Path from the hut and follow it between two little lakes whose stony shores and ledges support alpine plants, sedges, and shrubs. These botanical miracles possess the unbelievable tenacity of mountain flora, as long as nature's delicate balance remains undisturbed. Varieties of heaths, such as alpine bilberry and mountain cranberry, survive doggedly in niches of scant earth.

Beyond the second lake, on rising ground, the Camel Trail branches right to Boott Spur, and the Tuckerman Crossover leads to Tuckerman Junction above the ravine. Keep on the Crawford Path. It is well worn and marked by cairns, each topped with a yellow-painted rock. The gradual climb here is straight toward Washington's summit. The Davis Path joins from the right as you near the actual ascent of the cone. Not far beyond, the Westside Trail splits left to circle the cone for climbers heading toward the northern peaks of the Presidential

Range—Clay, Jefferson, Adams, and Madison. Watch for this fork and be sure to bear right; although the cairn markers are the same, there's no chance of confusion in clear weather.

Mount Washington's summit beckons 0.5 mile ahead. You pass patches of tough Bigelow sedge, which thrives in this exposed situation. Juncos also appear at home. Now you go up the cone in a passage among rocks. You climb the final shoulder and look away to the northern peaks. The Gulfside Trail comes in left from these peaks. You approach the summit from the north, up the last rock slope.

Your introduction to the modern age on the summit can be jarring—television towers, transmitter buildings, two monster cylinders rising like rocket launchers, a railroad with steam engine and passenger car, the occupants from the train and tourists from the auto road wandering around, the old stone-walled Tip Top House still preserved for its history—all appear insignificant compared to the extensive Sherman Adams Building partially encircling the actual summit. You are in the 60.3-acre Mount Washington State Park. The top of the world in northeastern America is a ledge behind the Sherman Adams Building, 6,288 feet above sea level.

Inside the commodious building you'll find shelter from the wind and wide views through windows that curve around the lobby-dining room. You can visit the cafeteria, gift shop, museum, and information desk. The Mount Washington Observatory, a weather station, is also housed under the roof of concrete slabs.

If you are lucky enough to reach the summit early on a perfectly clear day and are fit for the challenge of more above-treeline balancing on rocks, you may want to descend back to your car via the Gulfside and Jewell Trails. The total mileage for this hike is then 9.6 miles. (Or you may *climb* by the Jewell Trail. It starts from the Base Road opposite the hiker parking.)

The Gulfside Trail, which in sections could almost be described as paved with stones, takes you past the headwall of the awesome Great Gulf, the largest glacial cirque on Mount Washington. The Jewell Trail joins the Gulfside at the west slope of Mount Clay. Unlike the Gulfside, the Jewell Trail's upper section is composed of rugged slabs marked in yellow paint. Above the evergreen scrub, the trail is marked by cairns. Below treeline, the trail is a graded way, but don't attempt it in bad weather. While the views are magnificent, caution should guide your mountaineering on dangerous old Mount Washington.

Unless you choose the Gulfside-Jewell variation, descend as you came up, by the Crawford Path and Ammonoosuc Ravine Trail.

37

The Alpine Garden

Distance (round trip): 8½ miles

Walking time: 6½ hours

Vertical rise: 3,500 feet

Maps: USDA/FS 7½' Mt. Washington SE; USGS 7½' x 15' Mt. Washington

The object of the climb to Mount Washington's Alpine Garden is enjoyment of the mountain rather than its conquest. This loop climb, with the garden as its destination, is a rugged and demanding rock-scramble above treeline. But it's spectacular and shows you why the mountain is unique. The alpine-arctic environment at the garden affords more attractions than the tourist mecca on the summit.

Despite its barren appearance, this mile-high garden displays many of the 110 plant species that live above treeline on Mount Washington and other Presidential peaks. Of this total, 75 are never found below these altitudes in New Hampshire. Most of the alpine plants occur at lower elevations in Alaska, northern Canada, Greenland, and arctic Eurasia.

The flower-blooming time, mid-June to July, brings the Alpine Garden a miraculous shower of colors. Then you see yellow alpine avens, white diapensia, purple Lapland rosebay, and pink bilberry. The grasses, such as Bigelow sedge and three-forked rush, sprout new green blades.

The Alpine Garden's plateau interrupts Mount Washington's steep eastern slope. A curving, mile-long shelf between Tuckerman Ravine and Huntington Ravine, the garden begins and ends above these tremendous gorges. You look into dizzying depths and contrast them with the spaciousness of the sweeping views across Pinkham Notch to the Carter and Wildcat Ranges.

HOW TO GET THERE

The climb to this elemental world begins at the AMC's Pinkham Notch Visitor Center on NH 16, about 11 miles north of the junction of NH 16 and US 302 in Glen and about 10.5 miles south of the junction of NH 16 and US 2 in Gorham. Park in the parking area.

THE TRAIL

Walk behind the Pinkham Notch Visitor Center Trading Post to the Tuckerman Ravine Trail. Follow this trail for about 150 feet and watch on your right for the Old Jackson Road. This ancient wagon road is now a trail

and part of the AT marked as usual with the white blazes. It takes you straight through a junction with the Blanchard Loop and Connie's Way ski trails, across the Link Ski Trail, and past the Crew-Cut Trail and then George's Gorge Trail, while crossing several brooks before ascending to a sharp left turn off the old grade onto a trail cut in 1977. (This avoids any climbing on the auto road, which was formerly required.)

On rock steps the trail rises steeply for a short distance. Then you pass the Raymond Path on your left; it leads to the Tuckerman Ravine Trail. Next, at 1.7 miles, you come to the Nelson Crag Trail. Turn left onto it. (For

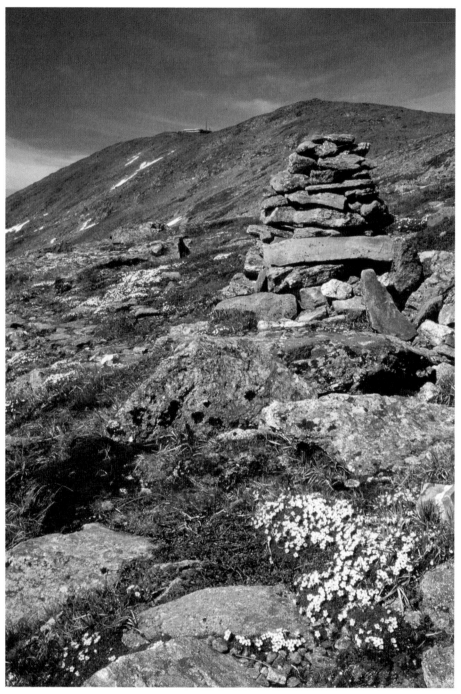

Alpine Garden

ROBERT J. KOZLOW

more information about the trail ahead and beyond the auto road, see Hike 33, Low's Bald Spot.)

The Nelson Crag Trail heads west and almost at once goes directly at the mountain. This steep section leads you for a mile through evergreens, which become scrub at an open ridge with views of Pinkham Notch. Turning north over rocks, it follows the auto road above the 5-mile marker and returns, left, to the rugged rocks on the side of Nelson Crag, which is not a single rock but a pile of huge rock slabs. A large cairn tells you that you've mastered the climb. Beyond the cairn you come to the Alpine Garden Trail between the auto road and Tuckerman Ravine. You are nearly a mile above sea level. (The Nelson Crag Trail continues beyond, bearing left across the Huntington Ravine Trail, over a rocky crest to crossings of the auto road and the cog railway before reaching the summit.)

At the junction with the Alpine Garden Trail take a good look at the weather. If you have any inkling that it will deteriorate in the next few hours or even if you are encountering ordinary clouds that are common above treeline, there is no point in continuing. The Alpine Garden is a gloomy rock field in cloud, and the cloud may be a warning of the deadly storms that blast Mount Washington. To retreat, turn right (north) on the Alpine Garden Trail and follow it to the auto road. Follow the auto road down to the Old Jackson Road for the return to Pinkham Notch Visitor Center.

But, of course, if you've picked a clear day for this climb, the skies are blue and the sun is dazzling. In that happy event, turn left (south) from the Nelson Crag Trail onto the Alpine Garden Trail.

Soon you descend over rocks with views of Huntington Ravine on your left and the cone of Mount Washington on your right. A great cairn marks the junction with the Huntington Ravine Trail. Keep straight across. (The Huntington Ravine Trail climbs right 0.25 mile to the auto road. To your left, it descends over the dangerous rocks in the ravine.) Now you are in the Alpine Garden, and ahead stretches the mile of scattered, broken stones among which grow the dwarf spruces, alpine plants, and shrubs. A pause for lunch gives you time to look about and absorb both the desolation and the life on this plateau, where plants not only survive but blossom in colors to match the rainbow.

(Warning note: Don't pluck or disturb the plants; they're unique, and they're protected. Don't drink from the little brook that crosses the Alpine Garden; it's contaminated by drainage from the summit.)

As you proceed, keep to the Alpine Garden Trail. Follow the cairns. The trail's worn rocks and tracked soil will guide you if a cloud descends—but pay attention. You cross a broad flat as you approach Tuckerman Ravine and the intersection with the Lion Head Trail. (The Alpine Garden Trail continues another 0.25 mile to the Tuckerman Ravine Trail.)

Turn left on the Lion Head Trail for magnificent views along the rim of Tuckerman Ravine. In June you will probably gaze down at skiers on late snow in the ravine. The trail leads you over Lion Head's granite brow to a descent of its bare eastern shoulder. You step down from reinforcing logs at frequent intervals as the trail curves to your right into evergreen scrub and the lower spruce/fir woods. At the junction with the Tuckerman Ravine Trail, turn left. The trail is a tractor road here, leading you 2.25 miles down to the Pinkham Notch Visitor Center, but the upper part is eroded to a bed of stones. If your legs are tired, don't try to hurry.

38

Mount Jefferson

Distance (round trip): 5 miles

Walking time: 5½ hours

Vertical rise: 2,700 feet

Maps: USDA/FS 7½' Mt. Washington SE; USGS 7½' x 15' Mt. Washington

The sensational view south from Mount Jefferson's summit owes its fame to a vast glacial cirque, the Great Gulf, backed by the towering crags of Mount Washington. A remote peak of the Presidential Range if approached from the north, south, or east, and the third highest at 5,716 feet, Jefferson conceals its western access under the spruces that grow in Jefferson Notch. There the Caps Ridge Trail leaves the road and surmounts a sharp, west spur for the short 2.5-mile climb to the summit. Caps Ridge, however, should be approached warily rather than with the assurance that you've found the mountain's weak spot. The Caps Ridge Trail ascends the equivalent of a vertical 0.5 mile.

The ledges, or Caps, challenge your legs and lungs. And the Caps present treacherous footing during or after a rainstorm.

HOW TO GET THERE

To reach Jefferson Notch, turn off US 302 at Fabyan and follow the Base Road toward the cog railway's base station. Drive about 5 miles to an intersection. Turn left there onto the Jefferson Notch Road (gravel). Careful driving takes you about 3 miles up to 3,008 feet. You are at the height-of-land on the road, where the Caps Ridge trailhead is the highest trailhead on a public road in the White Mountains. Turn into the parking area.

THE TRAIL

The Caps Ridge Trail leads east through green spruce/fir woods. Leaving behind this wet and rooty section, you begin the real

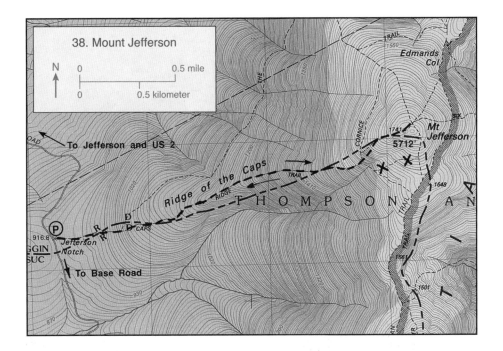

climb. Soon you catch glimpses of Mount Clay on the right.

About 1 mile into the hike the view opens at a smooth ledge, right, where small potholes in the rock indicate glacial action. Continue up 100 yards and pass the Link Trail on the left.

The evergreens get smaller as the trail rises steeply among jumbled rocks. You clamber up to treeline below the first of two jagged ledges called the Caps. About 0.25 mile above, as the ridge becomes a sawtooth edge, you climb the second Cap. You are exposed to all the mountains and the sky. You're also exposed to the weather. If you see signs of rain, fog, or high winds, turn back while you can.

Climbing on under clear skies, you descend from the last Cap and start up the broad main peak. At 2.1 mile you cross the Cornice Trail, which for a few yards joins your Caps Ridge Trail. (The Cornice Trail, avoiding Jefferson's summit, offers a rough route left, north, to Edmands Col. To the right it swings southeast and joins the Gulfside Trail.) Here on the mountainside, open to the most violent and frigid winds, grasslike sedges and rushes thrive in little slanting meadows among acres of broken rock. In the fall—August at this altitude—these green swaths change to soft, pale tan colors.

Above the Cornice intersection, you may guess the next rise to be the summit, but you climb over two more before the cairns lead slightly left up the summit crags. Now you discover that Jefferson's summit consists of three crests bordering a lower flat, where signs mark the trail junction.

Each crest gives you an interesting perspective across the Great Gulf toward

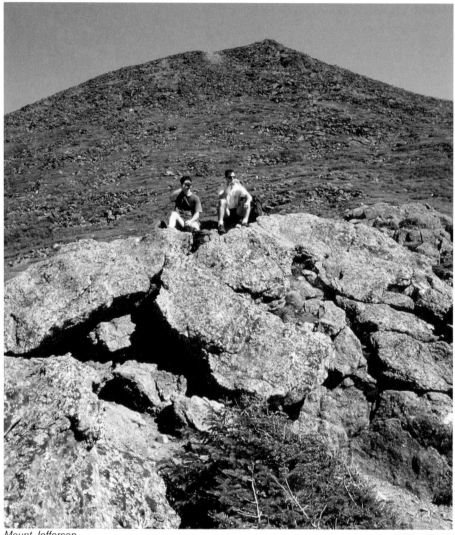

Mount Jefferson

Mount Washington, its auto road, and summit buildings. The southeast ledges overlook the Gulfside Trail's yellow-topped cairns crossing above the two ridges known as Jefferson's Knees. Looking east across Edmands Col to Mount Adams, you notice that it hides the last peak in the range, Mount Madison. (Note: The emergency shelter at Edmands Col east of Mount Jefferson on the Gulfside Trail has been removed.)

After lunch on the summit, return over the Caps down to Jefferson Notch and your car.

39

Mount Adams

Distance (round trip): 9 miles

Walking time: 7½ hours

Vertical rise: 4,500 feet

Maps: USDA/FS 7½' Mt. Washington SE; USGS 7½' x 15' Mt. Washington

Second in height to Mount Washington at 5,799 feet, Mount Adams fascinates and challenges many hikers more than any peak in the Presidential Range. It offers deep ravines and long ridges. Majestic views across the Great Gulf toward Mount Washington greet you from the summit crags. Mounts Jefferson and Madison seem like neighbors.

The shortest trail up Mount Adams begins at Appalachia, a former railroad flagstop that is now a parking space south of US 2. The Air Line Trail goes straight up prominent Durand Ridge.

HOW TO GET THERE

Take US 2 west from Gorham's traffic lights. Drive 5.5 miles over Gorham Hill and across the Moose River. You identify Appalachia on the left (south) by the row of hikers' cars even before you see the sign that says TRAILS PARKING.

THE TRAIL

Facing the mountains, take the path from the right corner of the parking area. Cross the Boston and Maine Railroad tracks. The path forks, with Valley Way bearing left and Air Line right. Keep to the right under the power line. At the edge of the woods is a sign for Air Line. You enter maple woods. Various trails, for which you have seen signs, begin to branch from both sides of Air Line. You pass the Link and Amphibrach. Next, you pass the crossing of Sylvan Way, then later, Beechwood Way. Then Short Line branches right,

39. Mount Adams

N 0 ⟶ 0.5 mile
0 ⟶ 0.5 kilometer

and you cross Randolph Path, all in the first mile. Keep on Air Line.

The trail goes up soon enough. Expect an abrupt rise beyond a spring on your left off the trail. The steep and uneven section of the trail takes you up Durand Ridge. You pass the junction of the Scar Trail coming in on the left, then after 0.5 mile you pass Upper Bruin; both trails connect to Valley Way in the valley of Snyder Brook.

Durand Ridge, reaching above treeline, sharpens to the Knife Edge. You clamber past rocks that overlook the precipitous King Ravine on your right.

From the ravine comes a trail, Chemin des Dames ("Ladies' Road"), which is the "easy" way up from that mysterious giant gorge named for its 1857 explorer, the Reverend Starr King. You look down upon rocks the size of houses. Hidden in caves under them, ice never melts. The ravine, by legend, is the resting place for a starving band of Rogers's Rangers, retreating after their retaliatory attack on the St. Francis Indian village in Canada during the French and Indian War.

Air Line next takes you past a branch trail, left, to the AMC's Madison Spring Hut, which is situated near the barren col between Mount Adams and Mount Madison. You keep on Air Line and climb steeply past the King Ravine Trail, right, at an entrance between ledges forming the Gateway into that glacial cirque.

Air Line joins the Gulfside Trail, coming in at the left, and they merge for a few yards. Mount Madison is in full view northeast.

(If you're caught by one of the notable Mount Adams thunderstorms, which feature virtuoso lightning bolts, and your hair seems inclined to stand on end, turn left onto the Gulfside Trail for a descent to shelter at Madison Spring Hut. Yellow-painted stones top Gulfside cairns.)

The Air Line Trail soon forks left off the Gulfside Trail. (Gulfside continues around Mount Adams toward Mount Jefferson and Mount Washington.) Air Line climbs past a minor summit on the left, named John Quincy Adams for the sixth president, and takes you up among rock slabs to the main peak of Mount Adams.

The summit spreads out before you a tremendous view into the Great Gulf. You feel as though you are leaning over the abyss, not because of sheer cliffs but because of the vastness. Mount Washington's superior height and size dominate the south outlook; the summit buildings are 3.5 miles away. Across the Gulf on a winding ribbon up the slopes, small bugs, which are cars, creep along the auto road. At the horizon to your right, Mount Jefferson stands jagged against the sky; to your left, Mount Madison. Turning around northward, you see below you a lesser crest, named for the revolution-ary of the Adams family—Sam Adams—and rising beyond is Thunderstorm Junction, where the Gulfside Trail meets other trails at a huge cairn. In this north view on a clear day, you see the two bare Percy Peaks in the distance and the ridges near the Canadian border. More to the east, Umbagog Lake sparkles in the forest at the end of Maine's Rangeley Lakes chain.

For your descent, retrace your steps down Air Line as far as the Gulfside Trail. Keep past the place where Air Line forks left and stay on Gulfside for the steep drop into evergreen scrub near Madison Spring Hut. The Gulfside Trail ends at the hut.

Take the Valley Way Trail for your return to Appalachia. Valley Way descends rapidly into the Snyder Brook valley and offers protection from storms after you enter the woods. Follow it past and across several trails until it joins Air Line, as you complete the loop and approach Appalachia.

Star Lake, between Mounts Adams and Madison

ROBERT J. KOZLOW

40

Mount Madison

Distance (round trip): 10½ miles

Walking time: 8 hours

Vertical rise: 3,800 feet

Maps: USDA/FS 7½' Mt. Washington SE; USGS 7½' x 15' Mt. Washington; USDA/FS 7½' Carter Dome; USGS 7½' Carter Dome

This rock pyramid completes the Presidential Range's northern peaks. Tourists and hikers alike see its bare crags towering above the northern approach to Pinkham Notch. Of its 5,366 feet, 4,500 rise directly from the Androscoggin River valley. It juts above treeline into the alpine-arctic environment of fragmented rock slabs, cold fogs, wind, and scanty vegetation. The peak is particularly impressive from NH 16 near the entrance to the Mount Washington Auto Road, where the Osgood Trail formerly began. Hikers for a hundred years enjoyed this scenic trail to Mount Madison's summit. They continue to do so, but from a 1985 parking area and an approach via the Great Gulf Trail.

Fine views on Osgood Ridge from treeline upward extend south and west into the Great Gulf, across to Mount Washington and along the range that sweeps over Mount Jefferson and Mount Adams to Madison. The route of this hike includes not only Osgood Ridge and Mount Madison's summit, but also the AMC's Madison Spring Hut and a return loop through Madison Gulf. The climb should be saved for a shining clear day.

HOW TO GET THERE

On NH 16, drive 1.6 miles north of the entrance to the Mount Washington Auto Road. Turn left at a large sign for the Great Gulf Wilderness.

THE TRAIL

With your pack equipped for a climb into the alpine-arctic zone, walk across the suspension bridge spanning the river. The trail

40. Mount Madison

N

0   0.5 mile
0   0.5 kilometer

beyond the bridge leads up a slight grade among hemlocks to the Great Gulf Link Trail from the Dolly Copp Campground, 2 miles north of your car via NH 16. Turn left onto the Great Gulf Trail.

Soon you will be walking above the rushing torrents and pools of the Peabody River's West Branch. At times the Great Gulf Trail coincides with sections of the Hayes Copp Ski Touring Trail from the campground. The ski trail is blazed with small squares of blue plastic, not to be confused with blue paint blazes of the Great Gulf Trail. Three bridges and skier logo signs accommodate your brook crossings and direct you. Stay on the Great Gulf Trail.

After a mile of this pleasant woods walk, your path bears away from the stream. You come to a junction of the ski trail branching north. In 15 minutes more you arrive at the Osgood Trail on your right, also northward. This trail will be your route to Mount Madison. (The Great Gulf Trail continues straight ahead.)

Turn right onto the Osgood Trail. You walk up an easy slope among beech and yellow birch, spruce and balsam. If you listen you can hear, in the valley, the West Branch pouring over boulders and into pools.

Before the Osgood Trail takes you to serious climbing, it crosses a small brook and then brings you to an important junction. On your left the Osgood Cutoff enters. Take notice because you'll return here as you complete your loop from the Madison Gulf Trail via this Osgood Cutoff. (On your right, almost under a big boulder, a spur trail passes a spring and ends at Osgood Campsite.)

Continue ahead on the Osgood Trail. You can start climbing in earnest. This steep section must be dealt with by the patience formula: one boot in front of the other. You climb through fine spruce woods. You're on a section of the Appalachian Trail, and you are also following the boundary of the White Mountain National Forest's 5,658-acre Great Gulf Wilderness.

The spruces diminish in size; they become sparse and scattered. You look up from your climbing and find yourself in the wind and skies among rocks that rise ahead, crest after crest.

Pause here and try to predict the weather. Fierce gales blast Osgood Ridge, and storms come up rapidly. It's a long, rugged, unsheltered mile over a series of high rock piles. You can easily turn back here.

Fair skies and breezes are the signal to continue to climb up the craggy peaks. Follow the cairns among the rock slabs and over the ledges. You are on the crest of Osgood Ridge, which curves left as well as up. You climb down a few yards over massive rocks to a narrow east-west flat. Trail signs mark this as Osgood Junction. The Daniel Webster–Scout Trail comes in on the right from the Dolly Copp Campground. On the left, the Parapet Trail offers a 1-mile circuit below Madison's summit to Madison Spring Hut.

The Osgood Trail goes up steeply again over the rocks along the ridge to Madison's northeast shoulder. It swings left down into a brief level section before the climb up the final pinnacle. On rising rocks again, you pass the Howker Ridge Trail, right. The Osgood Trail winds up westward among broken ledges.

At the summit, you stand on the big rocks that mark the end of the Presidential Range. The mountainside plunges northward into the valley. In that direction, the Watson Path drops off the summit. To the southeast you look down at the auto road entrance. Clouds may come pouring out of the northwest before you have studied Mount Washington and the cars rounding the auto road's corner, called the Horn, which you see across the Great Gulf. Mount Adams on the west often catches cloud wisps or disappears entirely.

Madison Spring Hut

The return route begins on the summit as part of a loop into Madison Gulf. Keep west on the Osgood Trail along the jagged ridge beyond Madison's summit. The trail, marked by cairns, bears left off the ridge and descends the shoulder to Madison Spring Hut below the looming crags of Mount Adams. The hut, where AMC "croo" members provide meals and lodging for hikers, serves also as a terminus for the Osgood Trail and various trails north and west.

Your route leaves the hut, south, by the Parapet Trail. Climb up the slope and keep left at the branch trail to tiny Star Lake. Across the col, the Parapet Trail makes a sharp left turn as you approach the lookoff ledges. Then it descends into a gully and the Madison Gulf Trail begins, right. (The Parapet Trail keeps on toward Osgood Junction.) Turn right onto the Madison Gulf Trail. Climb down carefully over the steep, slippery rocks among scrub spruces. *Warning:* The footing can be treacherous. Be prepared to take a lot of time.

The trail descends the Gulf by abrupt pitches between more gradual traverses, with many crossings of Parapet Brook. About 1.5 hours from treeline, you make the last crossing over the brook's smooth rocks, to the east bank, and climb to a trail junction.

Your route, the Osgood Cutoff, leads ahead toward the Osgood Trail. (The Madison Gulf Trail bears right down to the Great Gulf Trail.)

The Osgood Cutoff stays on a slabbing curve along the 2,500-foot contour through open woods. In about 15 minutes you'll see the sign for the Osgood Trail junction. Turn right down the now familiar route to the Great Gulf Trail, where you turn left and continue to retrace the morning's path. Avoid the ski touring trail sections. Watch for the branch trail to the right leading to the suspension bridge. Remember, the Great Gulf Link Trail keeps on to the Dolly Copp Campground.

Soon you can again admire the engineering of the bridge. Beyond it, you'll welcome your car and its four wheels to carry you.

41

Mount Kearsarge North

Distance (round trip): 6¼ miles
Walking time: 5½ hours
Vertical rise: 2,600 feet
Maps: USDA/FS 7½' North Conway East; USGS 15' North Conway

If you start climbing Mount Kearsarge North at dawn, and if the day stays clear, you'll see the shining wet rocks of Tuckerman Ravine's headwall 16 miles north on Mount Washington; to the right, Lion Head's cliff glows, and Huntington Ravine's rock facade catches sunlight in a bright chasm.

Maps show the mountain as Kearsarge North, which distinguishes it from the Kearsarge near the town of New London. (See Mount Kearsarge in *50 More Hikes in New Hampshire*, Hike 15.) The former name, Mount Pequawket, is all but forgotten. The Pequawket Native Americans hunted and raised corn in the Conway-Fryeburg forests and meadows along the Saco River.

Mount Kearsarge North became a popular summit for white men after 1845, when three enterprising men cut a bridle path to the 3,268-foot top and built a two-story wooden inn. The structure survived many years until an autumn gale blew it loose from its iron mooring rods and chains. Rebuilt, it stood for 25 more years before the winds blew it apart. A 1951-vintage fire tower now occupies the summit ledge, but like others in the mountains, it is no longer manned by a lone watcher; air patrols have taken over.

If you climb Mount Kearsarge North in the fall after snow has dusted the Presidentials, you'll understand the note on an 18th-century map issued during the French and Indian War, when this land was known only to hunters, trappers, and Native Americans. The note read, "These WHITE HILLS appear many Leagues off at Sea like great bright

41. Mount Kearsarge North

N 0   0.5 mile

0   0.5 kilometer

Clouds above the Horizon, & are a noted Land Mark to Seamen."

HOW TO GET THERE

Drive about 2 miles north from North Conway on NH 16. Pass the scenic outlook to Mount Washington. Cross the railroad tracks and turn right onto the Hurricane Mountain Road. Drive through Kearsarge village. Less than 0.5 mile beyond, the Mount Kearsarge North Trail starts on the left at a trail sign and small parking area.

THE TRAIL

The trail enters the woods and traverses tree-grown fields of the former Eastman farm; once a shady lane led to the house and barn. Steven Eastman built this lower trail through his pasture about 1872 as a link to the bridle path at Prospect Ledge. Now the farm has returned to forest.

The true ascent begins after the first 0.5 mile. Steadily upward the trail progresses through hardwoods of maple, beech, and birch to open rocks sparsely grown to sumacs and evergreens. You follow cairns and paint marks over slanting Prospect Ledge. There are views to the Saco valley south and west.

In the woods again, climb for another half hour along an ascending forest trail to more open ledges and scattered trees. Gradually you pass the minor wooded summit, Bartlett Mountain, on your left and swing north and east around ledges again. Turning south for the final climb, you follow cairns and worn paths up the last rocks among spruces to the summit ledge and tower. You first look straight ahead to Maine and its lakes. Then you turn left, and the Presidential Range takes all your attention.

To descend from the summit, follow the trail you climbed. A leisurely pace will show you many plants and trees that you could

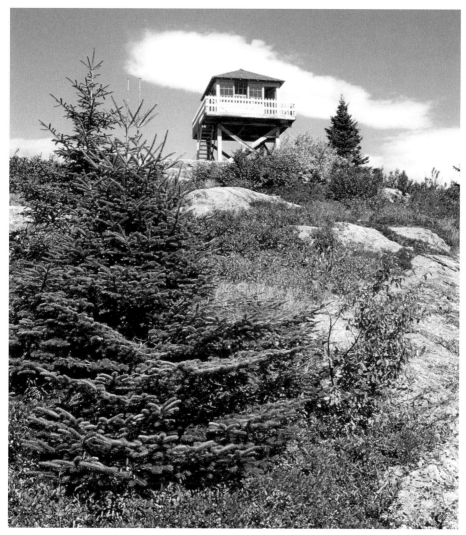

Kearsarge North fire tower

have missed in eagerness to reach the summit. First, the vines of mountain cranberry climb to crevices only a few yards from the tower. Soon, to the right, crowberry, another subalpine plant, creeps over hummocks in the scrub evergreens. During late June and early July, sheep laurel blooms pink and showy. Crumbled rock fragments support three-toothed cinquefoil. The trail offers examples of the predominant conifers in the White Mountains—magnificent white pines, red pines, balsam fir, red spruce, and the long aisles of a hemlock forest above the brook.

For full appreciation, Mount Kearsarge North requires several visits.

Mount Kearsarge North

42

Tom-Field-Avalon Loop

Distance (round trip): 8 miles

Walking time: 6 hours

Vertical rise: 2,800 feet

Maps: USDA/FS 7½' Crawford Notch; USGS 7½' Crawford Notch

Trails south from Crawford Notch link Mount Tom, Mount Field, and Mount Avalon for a loop hike. Spruces cloak Mount Field and Mount Tom, but both summits reach above 4,000 feet: Mount Tom, 4,051 feet, and Mount Field, 4,340 feet. Mount Avalon, a bare rock escarpment at 3,442 feet, overlooks Crawford Notch toward Webster Cliff and Mount Washington.

HOW TO GET THERE

The official trailhead parking for all trails in this area is the Crawford Path parking lot on the Mount Clinton Road, northeast off US 302 in Crawford Notch. To reach the parking lot from Twin Mountain, at the junction of US 3 and US 302 take US 302 east, and drive about 8 miles. If you are coming from North Conway, the parking lot is about 21.5 miles from the junction of US 302 and NH 16 in Glen.

Walk 0.5 mile along the Mount Clinton Road and US 302 to Crawford Depot to begin your hike. In the old railroad depot is the Macomber Family Information Center maintained by the AMC, which acquired the land and remaining buildings around the Crawford House after it was dismantled and burned in 1977. In 2003, the AMC's Highland Center opened on the site of the Crawford House.

THE TRAIL

Your loop hike will take you up the Avalon Trail to the A-Z Trail and Mount Tom Spur, then the Willey Range Trail to Mount Field, back down the Avalon Trail to Mount Avalon, and the return to Crawford Depot.

The Avalon Trail, your first section of the loop, begins across the Conway Scenic Railroad tracks south of the depot. It is blazed yellow. A wide path through the woods, it soon leads you past the trail on the left to Mount Willard, which offers less ambitious members of a party a spectacular view for 1.6 miles of upgrade. (See Hike 21 in *50 More Hikes in New Hampshire*.)

Shortly you come to the valley's brook and cross. Up the west bank you begin the real climb. You pass on your left the lower and upper junctions with the Cascade Loop Trail, which runs by Beecher and Pearl Cascades. A ledge farther on, and left, gives a breathing place above The Pool.

About half an hour from your car, the trail leads to the right, west of the old path lower on the bank, and takes you to the second crossing of the brook. You are climbing toward the steep end of the valley, which is essentially a glacial cirque with a wooded headwall. Many waterbars and steps have been built into the trail. Watch for the A-Z Trail. It forks right on an ascent where the upper rim of the cirque appears in that direction. Take the A-Z Trail. (You will return to this junction as you near the end of your hike.)

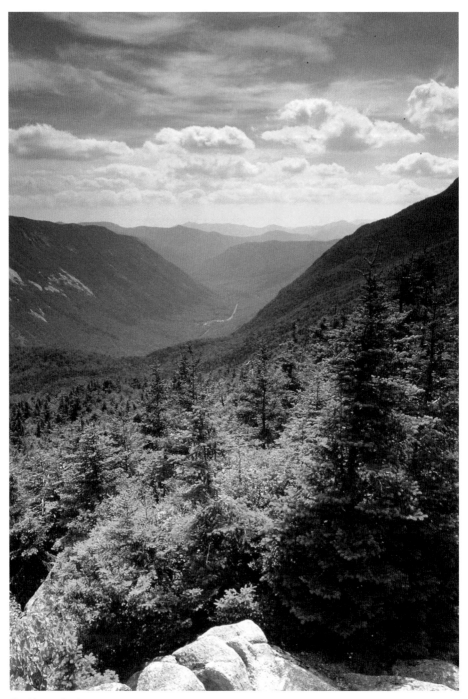

On Mount Avalon

The A-Z Trail drops into a rough gully and immediately climbs out to the right, then angles up for 0.5 mile to the last trickling brook. You begin the steep, rough 0.5-mile climb that takes you up to the height-of-land between Mount Tom and Mount Field.

A spur trail leads right for the 0.5-mile climb to Mount Tom's summit. It winds through a tunnel in the evergreens into leafy trees alternating with spruce and fir. Blown-down evergreens on the north shoulder are being superseded by birch and poplar. Near the summit, a side path to the right brings you to an open area of spruce/fir blow-downs, with a view southeast toward Mounts Field and Avalon. On the summit the view is of Zealand Notch. There are benches.

A quiet lunch among Mount Tom's spruces and firs may reveal dark spruce grouse feeding toward you among the ferns and wood sorrel or pecking at the evergreen needles. The male sports a red eyebrow. In sunlight and shade his black and gray feathers hide him until he moves. This denizen of remote conifer forests is protected by New Hampshire law. His deliberate actions and lack of fear caused early hunters to think of domestic fowl and name him and his mate "fool hens."

After lunch, retrace your steps to the A-Z Trail, and turn right. Follow it a short distance to the Willey Range Trail, which branches left toward Mount Field. (The A-Z Trail continues into the valley to join the Zealand Trail; thus its significance: Avalon to Zealand. For a description of the Zealand Trail, see Hike 31.)

Through close growths of fir, spruce, and birch, you begin the 1-mile climb to Mount Field's summit. You emerge into more open woods and taller evergreens. Keep on up the final pitch, passing the junction where the Avalon Trail descends, left. You reach the summit in another 100 yards. A small opening between dead or fallen spruce and fir affords a view south to North and South Twin Mountains and more distant peaks, as well as the nearer Zealand Valley, westward.

To the north you walk across the trail and look toward the panorama of summits south of Mount Washington—Eisenhower, Jackson, Webster, and Crawford Notch. Beyond Washington and its barren slopes below the buildings and broadcasting towers, Mount Jefferson looks more remote and unspoiled.

Return to the Avalon Trail for the descent. It drops sharply down the side of Mount Field through low spruces. Care should be taken here: the footing on broken stones, wet turf, and occasional mud is often treacherous, despite the stone and log steps. The flat shoulder leaning toward Mount Avalon's rocks provides openings in the scrub for views north and east. Behind you Mount Field rises so abruptly, you'll understand why you descended so quickly.

The main trail bypasses the crest of Mount Avalon, but a side trail leads to the right a few yards up the rocks for a bird's-eye view of Crawford Notch 1,500 feet below. Don't miss this lookoff because you are a bit weary. You'll see the highway parallel to the railroad winding through the notch, one of the great passes of the Northeast. Webster Cliff is a stark mass of sheer rock buttressing the mountain northward. In the distance you gaze at the long Presidential Range centered on Washington's barren cone, which you identify by the buildings and towers.

Below Mount Avalon, the trail continues to drop rapidly down through the spruces to the junction with the A-Z Trail. When you reach the Cascade Loop Trail, you might consider doing this loop. The cascades are a pleasant end to the day, and you can rest knees tired from the descent. Then continue to Crawford Depot and on to your car.

43

Mount Starr King/ Mount Waumbek

Distance (round trip): 7½ miles

Walking time: 6 hours

Vertical rise: 2,600 feet

Maps: USDA/FS 7½' Mt. Washington NW; USGS 7½' x 15' Pliny Range

A hiker in the White Mountains should see the Presidential Range from Mount Starr King. Thirteen miles northwest of Mount Washington across the upper valley of the Israel River, Starr King gives you a look at the complete panorama of the five rocky crests serrating the horizon eastward above the massed green slopes. From Mount Washington your eyes follow the skyline over Clay, Jefferson, Adams, and Madison.

In his 1859 book, the Reverend Thomas Starr King described the then-neglected views of the Presidentials from the north and northwest. He extols Jefferson "Hill," which he says "may without exaggeration be called the *ultima thule* of grandeur in the artist's pilgrimage among the New Hampshire mountains, for at no other point can he see the White Hills themselves in such array and force." The Reverend King gives no account of climbing summits north of present US 2, but his name is fittingly given to the mountain that is the great lookoff for studying and enjoying the northern slopes of the Presidentials.

HOW TO GET THERE

Parking and the trailhead are in the village of Jefferson, north of US 2. Opposite the Waumbec Golf Club, 0.7 mile east of NH 116, you'll see a hiker sign and a Starr King Trail sign. If you approach from the east on US 2, it is 3.6 miles from NH 115. Turn up a narrow gravel road at the signs. Keep straight uphill, avoiding the right-branching driveways to several large houses. You enter

43. Mount Starr King/Mount Waumbek

On Mount Starr King

the woods at a boundary sign for the national forest and soon reach the parking area.

THE TRAIL

The Starr King Trail leaves the east end of the parking area on an old logging road, then turns left to join the old trail. You climb through hardwoods, paralleling the brook down on your left. You pass the round foundation of an old springhouse on the right. The trail takes you up the mountain at an equable grade. As you climb into the zone of spruce and fir toward 3,000 feet, you pass a spring on the trail's left slope. The trail swings around to the north as it continues up and up. It approaches the summit from that direction.

Past the summit, proceed along the trail to a ledge for a view, and then continue into a clearing for another. There before you—peak after peak—are the Presidentials!

Sunlight alternates with cloud shadows over the mountains. Often, mists gather around the rugged peaks of Mounts Adams and Washington. Binoculars bring out Madison Spring Hut in the col between Madison and Adams. You look into the depths of King Ravine on Adams. Watch for the train on the cog railway climbing Washington. Below your vantage point is the green valley of Israel River and Jefferson Meadows, and farther away you see wooded Cherry Mountain. The Franconia Range seems far away beyond numberless smaller mountains and ridges, but Lafayette's blue-green silhouette assures you that you're looking at Franconia Notch's giant. Your gaze inevitably returns to the main attraction, the Presidential Range.

When you finally look more to your left, you notice a ridge eastward, where spruces rise to a wooded summit 1 mile away: Mount Waumbek, seemingly of no consequence. But a trail in that direction leaves from the southeast corner of the clearing below the site of the dismantled log shelter. It winds through the evergreens below the ridge, then ascends. Although roughly laid out among stumps and tree trunks, it is well worn by hikers adding another 4,000-foot mountain for their records. Mount Waumbek is higher than Starr King—4,006 feet against 3,907.

Waumbek offers glimpses of the Presidentials through spruces at the end of a short trail past the summit. Clouds whirl turbulently overhead and gather around Mounts Adams and Madison. The appeal of Waumbek is primitive, a north-country wildness occasionally animated by small birds in the spruces—boreal chickadees and golden-crowned kinglets.

The Kilkenny Ridge Trail leaves the summit of Waumbek for South Pond 20 miles northeast.

Return to the clearing on Starr King for a final scanning of the panorama before you, then descend through woods brightened by the lowering sun along the trail you climbed when the day was new.

44

Mount Eisenhower

Distance (round trip): 6½ miles
Walking time: 5 hours
Vertical rise: 2,750 feet
Maps: USDA/FS 7½' Stairs Mtn.; USGS 7½' Stairs Mtn.; USDA/FS 7½' Crawford Notch; USGS 7½' Crawford Notch; USDA/FS 7½' Mt. Washington SW; USGS 7½' x 15' Mt. Washington

Southwest from Mount Washington, rocky peaks extend toward Crawford Notch. One of these, Mount Eisenhower (formerly Mount Pleasant), commands a spectacular view to all points of the compass.

This broad dome overlooks sections of the famous 8-mile Crawford Path from Crawford Notch. Three beeline miles to the north, past Mount Franklin's long hump and Mount Monroe's two crests, Washington looms in its role as the highest point in the Northeast: it hosts tourists carried to the top by cog railway and automobile; it supports the summit buildings, towers, and observatory; it tolerates—with occasional good weather—the many hikers on its exposed slopes.

Into the arctic-alpine world of Mount Eisenhower, the Edmands Path climbs up a west ridge and around the north base of the dome to the Crawford Path. There, near this junction, a side trail leads up the crags and over the rounded 4,760-foot summit. On a clear day, from that vantage point high above the forests, the sky and rocks are elemental and clean.

HOW TO GET THERE

To reach the Edmands Path, turn north off US 302 at Fabyan onto the Base Road leading to the cog railway's base station. Soon Mount Eisenhower comes into sight as a hemispherical outline contrasting with its more jagged neighbors and identified by its above-treeline dome against the eastern sky. (The great cairn on the summit has flattened out in recent years. An easy way to identify Mount Eisenhower is to remember that it resembles

44. Mount Eisenhower

N

0   0.5 mile
0   0.5 kilometer

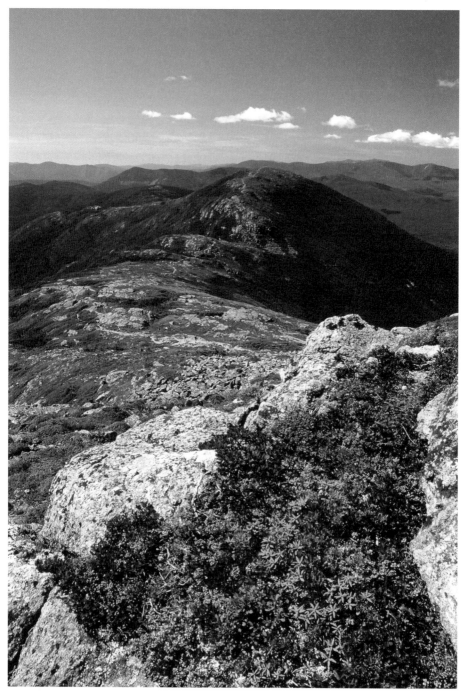

Mount Eisenhower

Ike's bald pate.) Drive on the Base Road about 5 miles to an intersection. Turn right. You are now on the Mount Clinton Road. Drive 1.5 miles from the four corners. And drive carefully; there's a startling 90-degree curve left about 0.5 mile from the trail.

THE TRAIL

In the parking area you'll see a sign for the Edmands Path. The great trail builder J. Rayner Edmands relocated and graded the path in 1909. It bears left among beech and yellow birch and crosses two small brooks on short footbridges. Then you'll cross Abenaki Brook on a bridge. Keep to the right up an old logging road beside the brook. You begin to climb somewhat here. The trail swings left up the ridge that will take you to treeline. The grade steepens but is nowhere excessive. You enter spruce/fir woods, the habitat of the blackpoll warbler and Bicknell's thrush.

You climb up sections of graded fill held on the slope by rockwork. You notice rocks drilled and split with hand tools to clear and ease the way. In the upper spruce/fir woods the trail crosses three seasonal source streams of Mount Pleasant Brook. Approaching treeline, you find the trail paved with flat stones. This improvement of Edmands's meticulous trail construction was a 1930s CCC task.

Halfway between a stone gateway and the end of the Edmands Path, look for a cliff formation that some hikers have dubbed a "mini Old Man of the Mountain."

If a cloud thick as sea fog masks the rocks, or if a storm threatens, heed the forest service warning sign in the last trees and turn back.

Once above treeline, you will see that the Edmands Path splits into three gravel trails between ledges and across the alpine sward. Keep straight toward the junction with the Crawford Path. Then turn right onto the Mount Eisenhower Loop, a side trail over Mount Eisenhower, whose rough dome rises ahead. (The Crawford Path bears left around the base.) You descend slightly and pass a little pool, Red Pond, on your left. Up the ragged ledges the trail zigzags, then takes you in a more gradual swing to the wide summit and the cairn. The green cushions all across the summit are the alpine plant diapensia. If you climb in mid-June, you'll see the array of white blossoms.

Be careful not to step on the plants as you walk around admiring the views. Stepping stones are plentiful. To the north, up Mount Franklin, curves the old and honored Crawford Path. Dropping away east of Mount Franklin, the ledges disappear into Oakes Gulf, where the Dry River (Mount Washington River) begins its turbulent run to the Saco River. Beyond Mount Franklin, you see a small peak on the left and a higher crest right, which combine to form Mount Monroe. Then comes Washington, often crowned by a misty cloud.

Your return follows the same route to the Edmands Path junction. Turn left down to the graded way and into the trees. The construction so carefully carried out by J. Rayner Edmands makes the descent nearly as painless as your tired legs will experience anywhere. But this ease may trick you: it's likely to lull you so that the descent seems longer than the climb.

45

Mount Crawford

Distance (round trip): 5 miles

Walking time: 4½ hours

Vertical rise: 2,100 feet

Maps: USDA/FS 7½' Stairs Mtn.; USGS 7½' Stairs Mtn.; USDA/FS 7½' Bartlett

A rough oval of ledges around spruce scrub, Mount Crawford's 3,119-foot promontory extends into the broad delta of ridges and valleys that flow 10 miles south from Mount Washington. Two great cliffs, 1.5 miles northeast, the Giant Stairs, identify Stairs Mountain and the long, forested Montalban Ridge. The Presidential Range's southern peaks appear at the far north end of the Dry River valley. To the northwest, Mount Willey looms over Crawford Notch.

A former bridle path, cut 15 years before the Civil War, passes east of Mount Crawford to Mount Washington. (A spur path rises to Mount Crawford's summit.) This route, called the Davis Path, was constructed by Nathaniel Davis, proprietor of the Mount Crawford House and brother-in-law of the famous Ethan Allen Crawford. Nathaniel Davis sold his horses about the time adventurous sightseers began riding up the Carriage Road being built from the Glen House in Pinkham Notch. After 1855 the bridle path fell into disuse and grew back to woods. In 1910, the AMC and volunteers reopened it, discovering, with the aid of a Maine woodsman, the entire original path.

HOW TO GET THERE

To make this historic and rewarding hike, drive about 6 miles west from Bartlett on US 302. Watch for a stone house known as Notchland Inn on the left above a railroad crossing for old US 302, now bypassed. This granite mansion was built in the 1860s by Samuel Bemis, a dentist who was also one of the first American photographers. A short distance beyond the inn, you'll see a Davis Path sign on the right. Turn right into the large parking area.

THE TRAIL

The Davis Path begins at the northwest corner along a rough roadway to the Bemis Bridge, a suspension footbridge over the shallow Saco River. Beyond the bridge, in an old field grown to bushes and trees, you skirt a wide lawn and house on your right. At a Davis Path sign follow the path, left, into bushes and alders. It leads you to a pair of logs over a muddy brook channel. At the opposite bank, turn right. You'll walk through woods and across a dry brook bed with

smooth stones, which takes the spring overflow from the running brook you soon cross.

You begin the climb along the old bridle path. The grade is steady, with occasional log or rock steps. You climb more steeply on straight stretches dug from the slope and supported on your left by rock retaining walls, which Nathaniel Davis built for permanence. You wonder at the strong backs and patience of the men who worked with oxen, chains, and crowbars. The graded trail reminds you of the untold miles of New England's stone walls.

You follow winding turns as you approach the top of the ridge. You emerge from spruces on open ledges, where you look

On Mount Crawford

northwest to Crawford Notch and Mount Willey. Keep right, over two wavelike swells and across an arm of spruce woods to rock again. Watch for cairns ahead and faded white and blue paint marks on the ledges among scattered spruces.

You come to a long, slanting rock face. Signs indicate the Davis Path continuing to the right and the Mount Crawford spur ahead. Walk up that rock face.

At the top, the trail proceeds among ledges and spruces, marked by a few cairns and faded paint blazes. The trail stays on the ridge crest, and about 0.3 mile from the Davis Path you step out on the cliff that looks off to the Giant Stairs and the gravel slides of Montalban Ridge. Ledges continue around a small growth of spruces, with views up the

Dry River—misnamed, because it can be a turbulent, dangerous stream—to Mounts Eisenhower, Franklin, Monroe, and Washington. Walk around and look southwest to Mount Carrigain and its tower. To your left, down in the valley, you see the stone house and the highway. Mount Crawford gives you a complete 360-degree panorama for your 2.5-mile climb.

Giddy from mountain vistas, you may for a change turn to the tiny cranberry vines clinging to rock crevices along with alpine crowberry. Labrador tea and blueberries grow in the shelter of the spruces. White-throated sparrows flit nearby. Cedar waxwings perch on dead twigs and survey the scene in their alert way. This is a place to linger, to look about again, and to eat a hearty lunch.

Backpacking Hikes

His pack was heavy but it made him feel free
and secure because it contained shelter and
food and everything they'd need in the woods.
It was like carrying a home on your back.

–Daniel Doan,
Amos Jackman

46

Mount Hancock

Time allowed: 2 days, 1 night
Distance (round trip): 9½ miles
Walking time (with pack for 5½ miles): 7½ hours
Vertical rise (including both peaks): 2,400 feet
Maps: USDA/FS 7½' Mt. Osceola; USGS 7½' Mt. Osceola; USDA/FS 7½' Mt. Carrigain; USGS 7½' Mt. Carrigain

Your first overnight hike should test, but *gently*. It should give you the chance to try out new boots, pack, tent, cooking kit, and food–and, most important, your own capacity. But it should not include too many miles. The trip to Mount Hancock meets these specifications.

HOW TO GET THERE
The Hancock Notch Trail goes north from the Kancamagus Highway at the hairpin turn about 10.5 miles east of Lincoln. Watch for a trail sign on the left. Just ahead on the right is parking at the Hancock Overlook.

THE TRAIL
Cross the Kancamagus Highway. The trail follows a logging railroad grade through hardwoods merging with spruce and fir as you swing east above Hancock Branch's North Fork. The grade curves around the west shoulder of Mount Huntington at about the 2,300-foot contour. In places, swampy ground nurtures lush sphagnum moss at either side of the packed fill. The rails have been gone since before World War I. Rows of blasted rocks still hold the fill in place. Cuts through ledge and banks are 10 and 12 feet deep. The fast, easy walking is interrupted at gullies and brooks once spanned by log bridges.

The hurricane of September 1938 laid down the trees that had begun to reforest the cut-over ridges and valleys. At the same time, Mount Hancock's north and east slopes were logged clear of all merchantable trees. For many years thereafter, the forest service closed off and kept watch over the area until the forest fire danger passed and

46. Mount Hancock

N

0   0.5 mile

0   0.5 kilometer

LINCOL

4403'
Mt
Hancock

FOREST

Hancock
Notch

Mt Huntington

×3393

Hancock Overlook

Kancamagus Hwy

To Lincoln

South
Sandpit

Trail Parking

HIGHWAY

Pemi
Overlook

new growth healed the devastation. The present trees demonstrate the rapid gains they make when protected.

The Hancock Notch Trail meets the Cedar Brook Trail, which branches left, northward, in spruce and balsam woods. You are 1.8 miles from the highway. (The Hancock Notch Trail continues east to the height-of-land and down to the Sawyer River, which drains into the Saco River south of Crawford Notch.)

Turn to the left across a little brook, and begin the climb up the Cedar Brook Trail. The name derives from the brook on the far side of Mount Hitchcock, which is ahead and to your left, west of north. Mount Hancock is ahead and to the right, hidden like Hitchcock by trees. You are still following Hancock Branch's North Fork. A bypass now spares you two of the five crossings. Along here you'll see trail erosion caused in 2011 by Tropical Storm Irene.

The brook takes on a rusty color. An old beaver pond, peat bogs, spruces, and tamaracks give the tan shade to the water. You follow the trail through a mossy bog where pitcher plants—those strange insect-eaters—grow near heavy turf interlaced with rootlets.

Watch on the right for the Hancock Loop Trail. It cuts into thicker woods as a wide aisle from the open, wet area and soon takes you across the brook to an overused campsite of bare earth, stone campfire circles—and, after rain, mud. Don't bother to look here for a place to pitch your tent. Seek your own site by continuing up the trail. It becomes a minor brook (sometimes dry) through jumbled rocks for a few yards. Next comes a boggy section. About 10 minutes from the overused campsite begin looking for your own private place.

I suggest as a landmark in a likely area the group of three big boulders to your left across the brook. Scout around above the big rocks or on the south side of the trail. You need only an opening large enough for your tent. Alternatively, you may climb farther up the trail as it rises above the brook and from there descend to level camping areas in the valley.

Along here you have carried your pack about 3 miles—far enough to have learned some packing tricks and trials, far enough to have felt, at least briefly, the exhilaration of carrying your home with you, the freedom of the backpacker.

The tent goes up quickly. Or it does if you've practiced in your backyard or even in your living room. Fluff out the sleeping bag. After you have cooked your meal on a backpacker's stove, as darkness approaches you may see white-footed mice hopping delicately near. Later, when you're dropping off to sleep, they will rustle in the pack's food bags if you left them on the ground, and you will have to wriggle out of your bag to hang the pack in a tree by flashlight, bare feet cold in the dew.

To avoid this, take precautions earlier. After your meal you should always remember to hang food 10 feet up and 5 feet out on a tree limb to protect it from animals, particularly bears.

Next morning after breakfast, prepare for a day hike. You have brought a little waterproof pack that can fold to envelope size when not needed for a day's excursion. In this, arrange sandwiches, raisins, candy bar, water bottles, compass, and jacket—not forgetting fly dope if it's early summer. Now you are ready for the trail, booted and ambitious.

Beyond your camp, the Hancock Loop Trail is still on the old logging road that parallels the valley on your left. The steady climb in hardwoods and evergreens lifts you up to glimpses of the slide identifying Mount Hancock's south slope. The Arrow Slide is a slippery-looking face of bedrock granite, at a distance smooth as gray glass above a jumble of rocks and gravel. Early ascents were made up the slide, a dangerous route now replaced by the wooded trail. You are now far

On Mount Hancock

ROBERT J. KOZLOW

above the brook. You come to the junction for the loop over Mount Hancock's two summits. To your left the valley drops away to a gully and the source of the brook—usually dry in summer—and to the base of the slide.

Both summits are more than 4,000 feet high, yet are wooded. To climb 4,420-foot North Hancock first—although the order chosen matters little—turn left down into the dry brook gully. The trail bears right, away from the slide's base, and enters the spruces. You climb up very steeply, but avoid the slide, as the trail is cut up through the woods. Despite the angle, much larger spruces once grew here. You may still see remains of monster stubs and fallen trunks, some charred from forest fire.

From the North Hancock summit, which you reach at an opening in the spruces, turn left to the head of the slide for a view toward the mountains around Waterville Valley, Mount Osceola, and some of the Sandwich Range.

Leaving the summit, the trail descends along the crest of the ridge and turns south-east on a narrow winding traverse up and down, around blowdowns, and across surprising wet spots. The trail gradually ascends South Hancock to its 4,319-foot elevation. An opening a few yards east gives you an outlook over the Sawyer River valley.

Beyond the south peak, the trail turns right, west, and drops sharply away down through spruce/fir woods to the end of the logging road that returns you to the junction where you began the loop. Of this loop, all but the ridge mile has been up or down as steeply as almost any trail in the mountains.

Retracing your earlier steps to camp, you have time for another meal before folding up the tent and packing for the hike out. Restore the site to its natural wildness, even to brushing up the duff flattened under your tent and sleeping mat; use a dead branch. And, of course, carry out all your trash.

For the return trip, an hour and a half should be enough—less, if you stride down the railroad grade like a veteran backpacker.

47

Sandwich Mountain

Time allowed: 2 days, 1 night

Distance: 13 miles

Walking time: 9½ hours

Vertical rise: 2,500 feet

Maps: USDA/FS 7½' Squam Mtn.; USGS 7½' Squam Mtn.; USDA/FS 7½' Waterville Valley; USGS 7½' Waterville Valley; USDA/FS 7½' Mt. Tripyramid; USDA/FS 7½' Center Sandwich; USGS 15' Mt. Chocorua

Viewed from a distance, the heavy silhouette that terminates the Sandwich Range's western reach contrasts with the much-photographed eastern pinnacle, Mount Chocorua. Sandwich Mountain rises massively from a broad foundation buttressed by ridges extending from Waterville Valley south to Beebe River and east to Flat Mountain Ponds. On the west, it slopes to Black Mountain above Sandwich Notch. Spruce/fir woods grow to the 3,980-foot summit, but ledges offer partial outlooks. On this hike, the climb up Black Mountain from the west provides the spectacular views lacking on Sandwich Mountain.

First Day: Sandwich Notch Road to Sandwich Mountain to Black Mountain Pond
Distance: 7½ miles
Walking time: 6 hours
This big day of the trip includes all your climbing.

HOW TO GET THERE
The Sandwich Notch Road is rugged. A four-wheel-drive vehicle is recommended.

From Campton, drive east on the Waterville Valley Road (NH 49) about 3.5 miles to a right turn, south, onto the Sandwich Notch Road. Follow this narrow, steep dirt road 3.8 miles to the Algonquin Trail, which begins on the left (northeast) side. If you are coming from the Center Sandwich end of the Sandwich Notch Road, turn at the Sandwich Notch sign in the village, drive along Grove Street, then bear left onto Diamond Ledge

47. Sandwich Mountain

N

0   0.5 mile

0   0.5 kilometer

Road, which leads to the Sandwich Notch Road. The distance from the blinking light in Center Sandwich to the Algonquin Trail is 7 miles.

Park in the small parking area and shoulder your pack. It should contain a tent; the shelter at Black Mountain Pond has been taken down.

THE TRAIL

The Algonquin Trail, blazed yellow, follows a logging road into the Sandwich Range Wilderness, crosses a brook, and branches left up toward the south face of Black Mountain. Climbing steadily among birches and beeches, it levels along the first bare rock and heath-like openings. Beyond a little seasonal brook you climb again abruptly to a col between a rocky knoll on your left and the main mountain ahead to the right. The next several pitches are difficult sections for the backpacker. In the evergreens you'll face one mass of creviced bedrock where you may decide to take off packs and pass them up.

The reward for this climb is a rocky lookoff into Sandwich Notch. The Sandwich Notch Road has been in use from the early days of settlement and once was bordered by farms and houses. From this viewpoint the trail turns back into thicker evergreens, then emerges onto open rock with scrub growth here and there on the ridge leading to the summit.

The Algonquin Trail continues to a junction with the Black Mountain Pond Trail coming in from the right. The pond is your destination for the night, so you will return to this junction, from which you now have a 1.7-mile spur that will take you over Black Mountain and up Sandwich Mountain. (Note: If you are getting tired or the hour is getting late, save Sandwich Mountain for another day and go directly down the Black Mountain Pond Trail.)

Continue east on the Algonquin Trail. It crosses a ledge from which you look down at Black Mountain Pond 1,000 feet below. Swinging somewhat left and entering spruces, you climb to Black Mountain's summit. Sometimes moose spend a winter on Black Mountain. Watching the trail and startled by droppings apparently left by a pony herd, you may not at first realize you're walking through a moose "yard." So dense are the spruce and fir trees that moose find winter quarters under the protecting branches and food from the evergreen tips. Snow, crusting upper boughs, roofs a sheltered stable for the huge animals.

The Algonquin Trail now descends to the ridge that leads to Sandwich Mountain. You pass occasional ledges and outlooks north, but mostly you ascend through spruce/fir woods. The Algonquin Trail joins the Sandwich Mountain Trail for the last few yards to the summit. (The Sandwich Mountain Trail comes in, left, from the Waterville Valley Road.) The spruces hide much of the view, but from rocks at the summit you get a lookout over Waterville Valley to Mount Tecumseh's ski slopes and Mount Osceola.

Retrace your route via the Algonquin Trail to the junction with the Black Mountain Pond Trail. Turn left, south, for the descent to the pond. The way is steep. Watch your footing and dig your heels in when gravity begins to get the best of you. The ledges and evergreens seem about to slide into the valley, yet they will probably stay in place. The tops of lower trees are on your eye level; you may have a close introduction to tiny golden-crowned kinglets. Approaching the base of this precipitous mountainside you descend through spruce woods that have never been cut. The trail levels out at beaver dams on the inlet to Black Mountain Pond. The trail swings around the west shore of the 6-acre

On Sandwich Mountain

Robert J. Kozlow

pond, which is 32 feet deep, clear, and the home of speckled trout. But don't count on a fish dinner.

Second Day: Black Mountain Pond to Sandwich Notch Road

Distance: 5½ miles
Walking time: 3½ hours

Easy walking this day leaves you free to swim and lie in the sun all morning. The pond is a gathering spot for birds and animals. Kingfishers, cedar waxwings, blackbirds, and ducks may be seen. In the spruces, white-throated sparrows flit about, and red squirrels scold.

You look back up the steep slope you came down and feel pleased that you don't have to climb it.

After lunch, pack shouldered once more, you locate the Black Mountain Pond Trail's yellow blazes above the south shore. The trail descends, crosses the outlet brook below rocks, turns right, and keeps to the east bank of the brook on a downhill slant along an old logging road. When you see a sign for Mary Cary Falls, take the short walk to this lovely waterfall. After about a half hour the Black Mountain Pond Trail crosses some low, wet ground partly spanned with bog bridges. Relocated around an area where beaver ponds may be abandoned or refilled, the trail again descends gradually. You step across the brook and turn sharply left, following the yellow blazes downstream to rejoin the logging road. Turn right and continue until another bypass, left, takes you around more boggy ground. This rough trail leads you to the crossing of the Beebe River, here a brook. On the far side, after a short distance, the Black Mountain Pond Trail ends at the Guinea Pond Trail. Turn right on the Guinea Pond Trail for the Sandwich Notch Road. (The Mead Trail, straight ahead at this junction, leads south up Mount Israel. See Hike 28 in *50 More Hikes in New Hampshire*.)

A shaded avenue, the Guinea Pond Trail follows the grade of a former logging railroad. It quickly bears left onto a detour path.

Depending on the season and beavers, there may be flooding in this open country of swamps and dams. The swamp on your right is also a thicket of typical bushes, such as withe rod and black alder. You pass a gate. The grade runs below a power line. You descend to another gate, and you've reached the Sandwich Notch Road. Turn right, north, over the bridge across the Beebe River. Follow the dirt road north about 1.5 miles to the beginning of the Algonquin Trail and your car.

48

East Branch Region/ Mount Carrigain

Time allowed: 3 days, 2 nights

Distance (round trip): 28 miles

Walking time: 21 hours

Vertical rise: 3,300 feet

Maps: USDA/FS 7½' Mt. Carrigain; USGS 7½' Mt. Carrigain; USDA/FS 7½' South Twin Mtn.; USGS 7½' South Twin Mtn.; USDA/FS 7½' Mt. Osceola; USGS 7½' Mt. Osceola; USDA/FS 7½' Crawford Notch; USGS 7½' Crawford Notch

A three-day weekend is ideal for this hike. You exchange your daily routine in the modern world for life in the remote Pemigewasset Wilderness between Crawford Notch and the Franconia Range. The pleasures of distant woods and high mountains, as well as the satisfaction of backpacking and hiking nearly 30 miles in three days, may escape you unless you've walked enough to toughen your legs. On the morning after the first day's 7-mile hike through Carrigain Notch, you'll want to rise from your sleeping bag eager for 13 miles of exploring the trails to Shoal Pond and Thoreau Falls. And you'll really enjoy the trip if your legs still have plenty of spring in them for the third day's climb up 4,700-foot Mount Carrigain.

For each of the three days, there are unique experiences to anticipate. First, Carrigain Notch, a true hikers' pass between mountain and cliff, opens to the headwaters of the Pemigewasset River's East Branch, where you camp near the site of Desolation Shelter, which has been taken down. Second, in those secluded valleys you find miles of first-class walking because old logging railroads provide easy grades beside clear streams. Third, Mount Carrigain's summit surprises you as a triangulation point for the great ranges, and the splendid panorama draws all the mountains together into a coherent pattern.

Mount Carrigain's tower on the third day is the hike's culmination before you descend to your car and to civilization.

Note: Tropical Storm Irene, which struck the White Mountains in 2011, caused problems on the Thoreau Falls Trail. There was bridge damage and a big washout midway along the trail.

Check at the WMNF Pemigewasset Ranger Station in Campton (603-536-6100).

First Day: Carrigain Notch and the former Desolation Shelter

Distance: 7 miles
Walking time: 6 hours

HOW TO GET THERE

You start your trip with a backpack into the wilds through Carrigain Notch. Drive west about 4 miles from Bartlett on US 302. Cross the bridge over the Sawyer River, and turn left onto the Sawyer River Road. There's a large parking lot on the left across from the start of the Signal Ridge Trail, which serves as a way to the Carrigain Notch Trail.

Note: The Sawyer River Road may still be closed to traffic because of damage done by Tropical Storm Irene. If it is, you'll hike an extra 2 miles from US 302 to the Signal Ridge Trail. Parking is available on the left of the entrance to Sawyer River Road. To find out the current situation, check at the WMNF Saco Ranger Station on the Kancamagus Highway in Conway (603-447-5448).

THE TRAIL

Shouldering your pack, you climb up the Signal Ridge Trail by a logging road across a brook and then across Whiteface Brook. On the other side, look carefully to locate the trail. As you climb the first ridge, Whiteface Brook pours through its little valley on your right. The trail swings west away from the stream, and you enter a logged area. Avoid the side roads. At 1.7 miles, the Carrigain Notch Trail forks right. The Signal Ridge Trail bears left. Turn right onto the Carrigain Notch Trail. (On the third afternoon you'll descend Signal Ridge Trail from Mount Carrigain's summit to this junction.)

Now you head north along the Carrigain Notch Trail and soon cross Carrigain Brook.

Again, you must search to locate the trail on the other side. The trail leads toward Vose Spur, which is ahead and to your left but mostly out of sight above the hardwood forest. The trail's route stays a considerable distance west of the brook. Two bypasses on your right approach the brook to avoid two beaver ponds on tributaries. Under Vose Spur your boots will teeter over rounded cobblestones of several dry washes from the mountainside—incongruous under the big trees but indicative of spring freshets.

At the base of the notch a clearing opened by a former beaver pond gives a view of the notch's cliffs. Keep to the left along a bypass around the debris left by the beavers. It takes you to the steep climb among spruces and birches to the pass at an elevation of 2,639 feet. You are entering the Pemigewasset Wilderness.

Wild and unknown to many travelers, Carrigain Notch forms a gateway to the East Branch valley. On your left, a towering shoulder, Vose Spur, separates you from Mount Carrigain's main bulk. On the right, Mount Lowell rises above the cliffs that complete the gunsight formation of the notch. The trail crosses beneath these heights among rocks and spruces.

Dropping down over rocks and roots, but more gradual than on the south slopes, the trail winds to an old logging road, which you can identify by rocks blasted into star shapes. The woods remain predominantly evergreens. You cross Notch Brook near its source and discover yet another bypass trail off to the left of the logging road's boggy sections. Pay attention. Your westerly direction is taking you north of Mount Carrigain and south of Notch Brook until you descend to a railroad embankment and a junction with the Nancy Pond Trail joining from the right. (The Nancy Pond Trail comes from Crawford Notch and US 302.)

48. East Branch Region/
Mount Carrigain (southern portion)

Former Desolation
Shelter Site

PEMIGEWASSET WILDERNESS

Norcross

Notch

Branch

Carrigain

WHITE

Carrigain
Pond

Carrigain Notch

Vose Spur

MOUNTAIN

Anderson

Mt

Mt Carrigain
4680'

Mt
Lowell

PEMIGEWASSET

SACO

Norcross
Pond

RD

WILDERNESS

Signal Ridge

SIGNAL

FOREST

TIONAL

Whiteface

Saunders

MOR

Brook

Brook

Brook

0   0.5 mile

0   0.5 kilometer

River

Sawyer River Rd

To US 302

Turn left for the continuation of the Carrigain Notch Trail along the railroad grade. For a mile you walk through evergreens, which open up at the site of vanished Camp 20 and a trail junction. The Carrigain Notch Trail turns abruptly right, downhill. Straight ahead and across a brook, the Desolation Trail begins. Its name refers to the devastation once caused by logging. (From this junction on the third day, you'll climb the Desolation Trail to Mount Carrigain's summit.)

Your first day's hike is almost complete, and it's time to consider camping sites. Camping is prohibited within 0.25 mile of the former Desolation Shelter, 0.2 mile away from the Desolation Trail junction, so you might want to camp back somewhere before this junction. Or you could choose a site at least 0.25 mile farther down past the Desolation Shelter site toward Stillwater Junction.

Meanwhile, you may rest or explore here at old Camp 20. It's typical of many deserted East Branch logging sites that have returned to woods. Built by J. E. Henry and Sons Company of Lincoln, Camp 20 remains only as rotted boards grown over by raspberry bushes. A dump hidden under forest duff contains rusty tin cans, old peavey ferrules, sled runners, and pieces of cast-iron stoves. In 1912 the clearing was alive with hustling men and horses working in the woods from daylight until dark. Trains carried away the logs. Now, most hikers scarcely pause in walking by.

One hiker did. He tells of discovering evidence of toil and poverty. Near the dump he unearthed a rotted leather boot that had been resoled four times. Nails held leather to leather on this relic, and attested to a lumberjack's "making do" his only pair of boots. Yet the hiker recalled that many old lumberjacks look back upon their younger days in the camps and forests as the best years of their lives. (Rough on the forests, however.)

Turn right at Camp 20 as the Carrigain Notch Trail heads toward the former Desolation Shelter. Situated among spruces, which provided its three log walls, the shelter opened toward a fireplace of rocks and a clearing above a boulder-strewn brook of transparent water—Carrigain Branch.

The water, however, may not be as pure as it looks. You've heard about the unfortunate exchange between humans and beavers—*Giardia lamblia*. (See Introduction.) One of Carrigain Branch's sources is a pond, Carrigain Pond, and therefore its water could be contaminated. For your drinking water, walk back up the trail and watch for the tributary on the left, north of its union with Carrigain Branch coming down from the south. This is the same brook you saw at Camp 20 and the beginning of the Desolation Trail. Filter or treat the water.

Because of bear activity in the Desolation region, use extra care when hanging food and cleaning up after cooking.

Second Day: Loop to Stillwater Junction, Shoal Pond, Thoreau Falls, East Branch, and back to the former Desolation Shelter

Distance: 13¾ miles
Walking time: 8½ hours

This walk along railroad grades and old haul roads benefits from an early start, which lengthens the day. Besides, as the sun begins to rise, you walk along the trail through cool woods; leaves and grass shine with dew, and the birds are singing.

For this loop you should leave your overnight equipment at your tent site. Set aside lunch, water, rain gear, and an extra shirt—your usual necessities for a day hike—in a little pack or fanny pack. Place all remaining food in a strong bag and hang it out of reach on a tree. Without your overnight equipment, of course, you also leave behind your backpacker's freedom. You might want to camp somewhere along the loop. If you decide to do this, evaluate the additional weight, and the mileage to complete the loop on the third day in distance and time, which I've not included. Mount Carrigain from the west is steep! You may want to stay another day if you treat the loop as a backpack instead of a day hike.

From the former Desolation Shelter the Carrigain Notch Trail goes 0.5 mile down to its end at Stillwater Junction. Here you will find three trails joining. On your right, north, the Shoal Pond Trail leads at once across Anderson Brook. It will be your route for the morning. On your left, south, the Wilderness Trail begins as a curving bypass of the railroad grade, which lies straight ahead, thus avoiding two river crossings once spanned by trestles, but now difficult if not impossible. (The Wilderness Trail then parallels the East Branch below Stillwater, on or above the south bank. It will be your afternoon's return route back to Stillwater Junction.)

Now from the spruces at Stillwater Junction you take the north route, the Shoal Pond Trail, which has become very overgrown, with many blowdowns. Cross the brook, aided by the concrete of a former dam. On the far side take the overgrown path that leads left for 40 yards (another path leads to the right but soon dead-ends), and just before it reaches a campsite look for a path leading to the right. It's completely overgrown for about 100 yards until it reaches the northbound railroad grade. Through the forest of poplar, wild cherry, white birch, yellow birch, and maple you come to the first crossing of Shoal Pond Brook. This is one of several bridgeless crossings in the 3.5 miles to Shoal Pond.

During logging days before World War I, standard-gauge steam locomotives chugged along the steel rails and crossties that were later taken up, rotted, or burned. The stocky, tough little locomotives towed flatcars from Lincoln with men and supplies for the camps and, when necessary as the trees were cut back, moved the camps themselves. The trains also carried Sunday excursionists, for a fee, and trout fishermen. The work trains returned to Lincoln piled high with spruce logs from landings along the East Branch and such tributaries as Shoal Pond Brook.

The Shoal Pond Trail takes advantage of one of these landings near the site of Camp 21. These platforms stored logs for the trains and were manned by a gang of men wielding peaveys. A cribbing of tree trunks supported J. E. Henry's landings against a slope above the railroad. The cribbing held the level rollway above the tracks where the flatcars waited. Horse teams dragged the sled loads from the haul roads to the landing and rested while peavey men rolled the logs off. Then the teamsters drove their horses back to the cutting woods. As many as 10,000 board feet of logs could be stored and rolled onto the flatcars below the landing. On the downgrade to the Lincoln sawmills, the flatcars shoved against the little engine. Brakemen scrambled over the slippery logs to primitive hand brakes. Link-and-pin couplings rattled, wheels clacked on rail joints, the engine chugged and thumped as it held back and blew out clouds of steam and smoke, as well as sparks that often set the woods afire.

The scene now at the site of Camp 21 is quiet and verdant. Only worn sled runners protruding from the leaves on the ground and cans from a dump show that the camp ever existed. To the right in the brook a large, shallow pool collects water flowing over a nearly level ledge. Upstream the railroad grade ends, and you cross to the east bank. You follow old sled roads over log corduroy or often on modern trail walkways of split logs. The Shoal Pond Trail has been taking you through the eastern section of the Pemigewasset Wilderness.

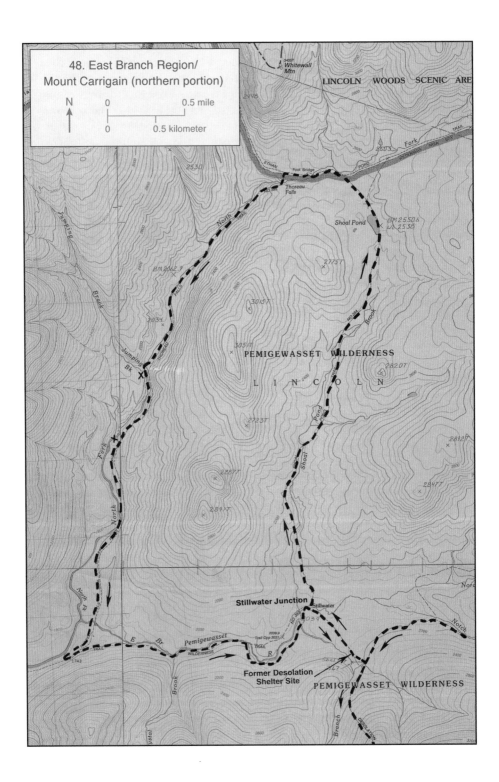

48. East Branch Region/
Mount Carrigain (northern portion)

N

0   0.5 mile

0   0.5 kilometer

LINCOLN WOODS SCENIC ARE

Whitewall
Mtn

Foot Bridge

Thoreau
Falls

Shoal Pond

BM 2550.6

PEMIGEWASSET WILDERNESS

L I N C O L N

Stillwater Junction

Stillwater

E Br Pemigewasset
WILDERNESS TRAIL

Former Desolation
Shelter Site

PEMIGEWASSET WILDERNESS

A young forest grows on the earth scorched by logging and fire. You walk in the shade of innumerable trees. Under national forest protection since the early 1930s, this East Branch country has made a miraculous recovery. The wonder of returning forest speaks loud and clear for conservation, yet might suggest to the thoughtful hiker that earth and nature have given man more reprieves than he deserves.

Crossing to the west bank of the brook, you are approaching the pond through evergreens. The trail curves eastward again into more open country. Corduroy logs have been preserved by the cold and acid bog water. The land rises to dry ground. Midway on the east shore of the pond you can walk from the spruces to the water's edge for a view of Whitewall Mountain and Zeacliff to the north. Not much of Mount Bond is visible anymore.

A few hundred yards beyond the pond, the trail splits. Both forks lead to the Ethan Pond Trail. Take the left fork, which follows the old Zealand Notch railroad grade. This was another J. E. Henry enterprise that ended with fierce fires in 1886. Burned to bedrock, Whitewall Mountain north of you stands as testimony to the blazing inferno.

About 0.75 mile from Shoal Pond, you reach the Ethan Pond Trail, where the Shoal Pond Trail ends. Keep left onto the Ethan Pond Trail.

For the purpose of this hike, the Ethan Pond Trail provides a 0.5-mile transfer to the Thoreau Falls Trail. (The Ethan Pond Trail comes from US 302 in Crawford Notch.) You follow the Ethan Pond Trail along the railroad grade to a footbridge over the East Branch's North Fork. Next, after about 0.25 mile, you come to the Thoreau Falls Trail on your left. This is your 5-mile return route south along the North Fork into the East Branch valley. (The Ethan Pond Trail goes north through Zealand Notch to the Zealand Trail near the AMC's Zealand Falls Hut.)

Take the Thoreau Falls Trail, left. You are in a Forest Protection Area: no camping or fires. Descending to the ledges and the brook, you find an ideal lunch spot. Thoreau Falls and noontime come together if the day's hike is proceeding on schedule. The North Fork cascades down the slanting rock into a deep ravine. Named, of course, for the author of *Walden,* the white water glints in the sun and is visible to hikers on the western ridge, where Mount Bond, the highest summit in the area at 4,698 feet, extends north to Mount Guyot, and Zealand Ridge curves along the northern horizon to Zeacliff.

After lunch you will have 7.5 miles of afternoon walking back to the former Desolation Shelter. The Thoreau Falls Trail continues from the steep bank beyond the head of the cascade. Care and caution are required due to slippery rock. Sometimes the flow of water will force you to retreat upstream in search of a less dangerous crossing.

Once on the far side you climb the bank, then pick your way down a precipitous, muddy, rooty drop as the trail descends into the ravine. The trail remains rough along the east side of the valley until you come to the sled road used by J. E. Henry and Sons' loggers when they began cutting the first-growth spruce in 1916. The trail improves as the valley opens out, and notably so when it meets the end of the old railroad grade and follows it.

This easy walking lasts about 2 miles. Watch on the left for the former high-water bypass. It is now the main trail and avoids difficult stream crossings. If you follow the grade to the North Fork you have gone too far by about 200 yards. The trail climbs the steep east slope. Its difficulty is preferable to negotiating (if possible) North Fork, Jumping Brook, and North Fork a second time to regain the grade.

Historically, this is an interesting area. The forest has reclaimed the old loggers' camps and railroad trestles. On the west bank below Jumping Brook there is a memorial plaque commemorating the deaths of Dr. Miller and Dr. Quinn of Hanover after a plane crash in February 1959.

The trail, ascending above an old landslide, swings south—parallel to the North Fork, but high up—before taking you down to the railroad grade once again. Turn left onto it.

Now you're all set for an hour's easy walking to the East Branch and a footbridge laid on 60-foot logs. (This bridge was damaged by Tropical Storm Irene in 2011. Eventually it may be removed to conform to Wilderness status.) Beyond this crossing you'll think the trail is leading you away from your correct eastern, upstream direction back to the former Desolation Shelter. It is. The trail follows the railroad grade for almost 0.5 mile southwesterly to meet the Wilderness Trail. Stay alert for this junction.

Turn sharply left onto the Wilderness Trail. The slope is gradual, yet seems steep for an engine with cars behind it. After about 15 minutes the trail leaves the grade to stay on the south bank instead of crossing as the railroad once did. This bypass winds along the bank and through Crystal Brook, then down to the grade, which has returned to the south near the clearing at the site of Camp 18. Past the field of grass and fireweed some distance south of the East Branch, the trail stays on the grade as far as the riverbank where the railroad crossed. You need not. A more recent section of the Wilderness Trail takes you around two former difficult crossings. Stay on the grade to its end and step into the woods by this trail. It curves to the south of Stillwater, crosses Carrigain Branch, and returns you to Stillwater Junction for the completion of your day's loop. Turn to the right onto the Carrigain Notch Trail, and retrace your morning walk to your tentsite.

Third Day: Mount Carrigain via Desolation Trail and Signal Ridge Trail

Distance: 7½ miles
Walking time: 6½ hours

If the weather is fair on this day of the climb up Mount Carrigain, you are in luck. If clouds and rain have descended, I suggest you go back to your car through Carrigain Notch and save the mountain for a clear day. You can see the summit from the brook bed above the shelter site. Take a look and make your decision.

Shoulder your pack, and walk up the Carrigain Notch Trail to the corner and junction at the site of Camp 20. Blue sky and sun overhead, turn right and you're on the way to Carrigain's summit on the Desolation Trail. (Clouds and rain up there, turn left on Carrigain Notch Trail.) Step across the brook. This is the last water.

You begin to walk on your trip's final railroad grade. It was a short spur track from Camp 20 to a landing at the base of the mountain. The Desolation Trail leaves it and heads up steeply before the embankment that appears to have been the landing and main sled road from the area around Carrigain Pond. Thereafter, the trail follows and crosses up between connecting logging roads as you surmount the ridge.

These former roads have thick bands of trees growing along them. Seen from a distance in the East Branch valley or from heights such as Mount Bond, they look like encircling, heavier-green contour lines in the second-growth forest. Known to loggers as "dugway roads," these were literally dug into the mountainside to support heavy sled loads in winter when teams hauled logs down to the railroad landings. The highest

Mount Carrigain

ROBERT J. KOZLOW

roads of J. E. Henry's operations were winter tracks using brush and side logs as "bunters" to keep the lighter sled loads from slipping off the steep slopes.

The Desolation Trail takes you to the end of the uppermost road, where the steepest ascent begins. This angle stopped J. E. Henry's logging, not because it was difficult but because it was unprofitable. Shrewd assessment of cost saved the present virgin forest bordering the Desolation Trail's top 0.5 mile to the summit. As a climber, you may also ponder the angle, but the slow upward pace will encourage you to enjoy the trees. The summit is 2 miles from Camp 20, wooded with low spruces and overlooked by the tower, which is no longer a glassed fire lookout but a viewing platform above the evergreens for hikers.

The views on a clear day extend for miles in all directions. You can trace the route of your previous day's hike northwest of the summit. You look across the great country preserved in the Pemigewasset Wilderness. More distant mountains surround it. The Franconias rise on the horizon to the west, and the Presidentials northeast. Mount Hancock is a near neighbor on the southwest, while southward Tripyramid and the Sandwich Range complete the circle.

Now the time has come to descend to where you started on the first day. You have 5 miles to go, and Signal Ridge will give you one more outlook.

The Signal Ridge Trail drops off the summit past the fire lookout's cabin site and well—which may have water in it, but treatment is necessary. The trail continues the steep descent to Signal Ridge. There you bear left along the crest for a fine view across Carrigain Notch to the cliffs on Mount Lowell. After abrupt downward progress, the trail slabs through a logged valley, passes Carrigain Notch Trail coming in left, and goes on down to the Sawyer River Road and your parked car.

49

Mount Isolation

Time allowed: 3 days, 2 nights

Distance (round trip): 14 miles

Walking time: 11 hours

Vertical rise: 3,200 feet

Maps: USDA/FS 7½' Jackson; USGS 15' North Conway; USDA/FS 7½' Stairs Mtn.; USGS 7½' Stairs Mtn.

A high ridge to separate you from the highway, a long wooded valley with a clear stream, miles of white birches, and a remote, 4,003-foot peak south of Mount Washington—these all appear for your enjoyment on your way to the summit of Mount Isolation. You follow the Rocky Branch Trail (named for the stream it follows, a tributary of the Saco River), the Isolation Trail, and the Davis Path on this woodsy three-day hike. Because you return by the same route, you have the opportunity to see again the trees and brooks and views you passed hiking in; this double exposure reveals new secrets and discoveries.

Your pack should include a tent. Because it is in the Presidential Range–Dry River Wilderness, where structures are prohibited, the Rocky Branch Shelter Number 2 is scheduled to be removed. Isolation Shelter has been taken down.

Caution: This trip should be avoided in wet weather. Trails hold water, and the five crossings of Rocky Branch can be difficult or dangerous.

First Day: NH 16 to Rocky Branch and Isolation Trail

Distance: 3½ miles
Walking time: 3 hours

HOW TO GET THERE
Drive north 5.5 miles on NH 16 from Jackson's covered bridge toward Pinkham Notch. Past a bridge over the Ellis River and beyond a White Mountain National Forest sign, right, turn left for the Rocky Branch Trail parking up an asphalt roadway.

THE TRAIL

The Rocky Branch Trail begins at the north end of the parking area. It heads uphill and soon joins an old logging road angling left up the slope. This route, opened in 1933, was a CCC project. I recall the piles of brush left by the crews and the stumps from trees that had grown in after horse-logging days.

The trail takes you up west and north from the highway in a forest of beech and yellow birch. About 10 minutes from your car the Avalanche Brook Ski Trail joins, left, marked with blue blazes. Look behind you to make sure you don't take the ski touring trail when you return. It coincides with the Rocky Branch Trail for a few hundred yards, then bears right across a small stream. (By now you understand the usefulness of the old woodsman's trick of looking behind for the return perspective.) Keep to the left, away from the logging road, as your route zigzags up to another logging road and to switchbacks often root-tangled and rocky.

Rising steadily up this unremitting series of slopes for 2 miles, the trail approaches the spine of Rocky Branch Ridge, but there's wet footing ahead. A left corner, westward, takes you to another ancient logging road down a slight incline, which levels across an area of springs and two streams that form Miles Brook. The trail ascends again. Spruce/fir woods begin at this elevation near the 3,000-foot sag in the main ridge, which attains 3,660 feet at an unnamed summit to the right of the trail. Across a muddy height-of-land you can avoid some of the boot-churned bog by taking an unofficial bypass left through the evergreens, and back to the trail. It dries out somewhat as you come to a sign for the wilderness area you are about to enter—the Presidential Range–Dry River Wilderness. Beyond this sign, camping must be at least 200 feet from streams, trails, and former campsites.

Descending the ridge, the trail is sometimes a running rivulet. The rounded rocks, eroded from the thin soil as far back as the days when this was first a sled road, are hazards to your footing. Occasionally, through the trees, you can see across the Rocky Branch valley to Montalban Ridge, but there's difficulty in identifying summits along it, such as Mount Davis and Mount Isolation. The trail improves greatly when it crosses a trickle of water to the left and takes to a logging road dug from the slope. This eases your way down to Rocky Branch.

There's no footbridge to take you across to the Isolation Trail, which is your upstream hike for the second day. This crossing can be dangerous at high water. An alternative is to bushwhack upstream on the east bank to pick up the Isolation Trail after its first crossing. In dry weather you can usually stay on the Rocky Branch Trail by stepping from rocks in the stream to a ledge above pools. Atop the bank beyond the ledge, the Isolation Trail begins on the right. Turn sharply left and follow the Rocky Branch Trail along the old railroad grade for 100 feet. The Rocky Branch Shelter No. 2 (or its site after removal) is in a little clearing above the stream. You may seek a campsite in the vicinity, but be sure it's 200 feet from the trail, stream, clearing, and any other obviously used camping place.

Second Day: Rocky Branch to Mount Isolation

Distance: 4½ miles
Walking time: 3½ hours

Your morning hike up Rocky Branch follows the Isolation Trail from the junction just north of the site of Rocky Branch Shelter No. 2. The trail turns left up from the railroad grade until, regaining the grade, it follows that route wherever possible but avoids slides and

49. Mount Isolation

N

0   0.5 mile
0   0.5 kilometer

To Jackson

To Pinkham Notch

Ellis River

Rocky Branch

COOS CO
CARROLL CO

Isolation Trail

Davis Path

Mt Isolation

Engine Hill

Mt Davis

washouts. A forest of white birches has taken over the blueberry barrens of years ago. Under the birches, hobblebushes spread broad leaves that shade the fern fronds and the fanlike leaves of wild sarsaparilla. The valley has seen many changes: spruce logging, then the fires of 1914 and the scorched earth they brought, blueberry bushes, sprouting poplar and wild cherry growth, and now tall white birches where the old spruces grew.

The Isolation Trail goes up the valley of Rocky Branch for about 1.75 miles, with four stream crossings, two of which are only 100 yards apart. The old railroad trestles went up in flames or rotted away, so you must choose stones to step on or wade with a staff. Occasional sections of the trail keep to the side of the hill on the east bank for rough but somewhat drier footing above the stream. Large boulders here and there interrupt the flowing water and form pools below alder thickets. You walk in a long grove of white birches.

Beyond the final crossing to the west bank, the trail leads into spruces and over damp ground along a tributary brook. As the flow of water dwindles you should consider selecting a place for your tent. Although the tributary stream you're following can be said to have its source near the site of the former Isolation Shelter, the spring, which supplied hikers, has sometimes been dry. I suggest you set up your tent now—of course, 200 feet away from the trail and stream and in a spot never used by other hikers. And don't drink the water without boiling or using another treatment.

Then continue up the Isolation Trail to the Davis Path. At this junction you have reached an elevation of about 3,800 feet. Clear skies on this second day of your trip mean that you should keep on to Mount Isolation. You are only a mile from its summit off the Davis Path

to the south. If clouds and rain envelop the junction, you may very well postpone the remainder of your hike until morning and possible fair weather.

The Isolation Trail heads north, coinciding with the Davis Path for 0.25 mile before it forks west and descends to the Dry River Trail. The Davis Path extends between US 302 in Crawford Notch, 11 miles south, and Mount Washington, an extremely rugged, mostly exposed 4.5 miles. (For the section of the Davis Path near US 302, see Hike 45, Mount Crawford.)

Take the Davis Path south. It soon passes the site of Isolation Shelter. A brief description of the old log shelter will pay tribute to its solidity, its usefulness of 50 years since I first slept in it (and it was older than that), but more especially to its architecture. A log cabin with an open gable end facing the fireplace on a huge rock, it was a more comfortable shelter than the common Adirondack type with overhanging front eaves. A campfire reflected back inside, to both the lower and upper bunks. Isolation Shelter never trapped smoke as do the open-fronts with low eaves. You never knocked yourself silly forgetting to duck as you went out. It always suggested to me a simpler and more primitive time in the mountains.

The trail climbs a spruce ridge overlooking Rocky Branch valley, left. But keep your eye on the trail. Watch for a spur trail, right. You scramble up a long 100 yards through spruce scrub to the flat, rocky summit of Mount Isolation.

The spruce scrub offers no obstacle to the outlook as you step across the ledges. The western horizon at once draws and holds your attention. The southern peaks of the Presidential Range begin in the south near Crawford Notch at Mount Jackson and extend north to Clinton, Eisenhower, Franklin, and Monroe, in a long serrated array to the great peak of Washington, which strikes into the sky 4 miles north of you. Mount Isolation places you high between two valleys that sweep down from Mount Washington to Crawford Notch; the line of summits, near whose northern end you stand, is named Montalban Ridge. You have hiked the Rocky Branch valley to the east; to the west and below the southern peaks, you look into Dry River valley, which isn't dry. Its upper waters are apparent as cascades on the headwall of Oakes Gulf between you and Mounts Monroe and Washington. (Dry River can quickly become a raging torrent. It bears another, more appropriate name: Mount Washington River.)

Mount Isolation is a grandstand seat for cloud shows. Often, white wisps and tumbling fogs swirl among the southern peaks. On some bright, clear days, storm clouds suddenly mass around Washington's cone and obscure the buildings and towers. If the storm threatens rain on Mount Isolation, retreat to your tent. Retrace your way east down the spur trail, and turn left onto the Davis Path. The site of Isolation Shelter is 20 minutes away. Turn right onto the Isolation Trail for the protection of the tent you've pitched away from the tributary to the Rocky Branch.

Third Day: Davis Path–Isolation Trail Junction to NH 16

Distance: 6 miles
Walking time: 4½ hours

Perhaps this morning brings clear skies after a previous rainy afternoon that kept you from Mount Isolation. You still have time to go up it, because this third day's hike is almost as moderate as the previous days'.

If you're early enough to Mount Isolation, you'll see the sunrise brightening Mount Washington, or maybe a shining white cloud around the peak. If rain pours down this morning, and you really want to reach the summit, you'll just have to slog along through the downpour. You'd be wiser to wait for another chance. There's nothing to see on Mount Isolation in a rainstorm except spruce scrub, ledges, Labrador tea, and mountain cranberry.

For the return hike, walk back down the Isolation Trail to Rocky Branch and then down the stream to the junction with the Rocky Branch Trail. Turn left onto the Rocky Branch Trail, cross the stream, and climb over the ridge. Then it's all downhill to NH 16 and your car—but avoid the ski touring trail, and turn right off the logging road just above the parking area.

50

The Mahoosuc Range

Time allowed: 7 days, 6 nights

Distance: 33 miles

Walking time: 32 hours

Vertical rise: 8,600 feet*

Maps: USGS 7½' Berlin; USGS 7½' Shelburne; USGS 7½' Gilead (ME); USGS 7½' Old Speck Mtn. (ME)

*This is an estimate based on map contour counting; the rises are frequent.

For many years the Mahoosuc Range was little known except to the "through-hikers" of the Appalachian Trail, who said it was the toughest 30 miles between Maine and Georgia. This route is federally protected as a segment of the Appalachian National Scenic Trail. In recent years, the Mahoosuc Initiative, which includes the Mahoosuc Land Trust, the Androscoggin River Watershed Council, the Northern White Mountain Chamber of Commerce, and the Northern Forest Alliance, has been working to conserve the region.

The town of Gorham and the Androscoggin River separate Mount Madison and Mount Moriah from the westernmost mountain of the Mahoosucs, Mount Hayes. The AT, descending from Mount Moriah south of the Androscoggin, crosses at Shelburne, east of Gorham on US 2. The AT follows the Centennial Trail toward Mount Hayes for the first 3.75 miles of this 33-mile backpack over the summits of the range to Grafton Notch and ME 26 north of Newry, Maine. From Mount Hayes the AT follows the AMC's Mahoosuc Trail.

The distance as the crow flies is only 18 miles. Allowing for the walking distances to ascend and descend at the ends of the range, and a southerly swing and some zigzags from peak to peak, the extra miles are up and down along the range.

The varied worlds along the way include hardwood forests, mountain meadows, spruce-shaded slopes, subarctic barrens, frequent ledges, sharp ravines, and summit after summit. The Mahoosucs are a unique experience. Leisurely travel enhances the experience; the Mahoosucs deserve a week. Of the seven days allotted, you hike six days, with time to relax at intervals and still make camp long before dark. One day is a spare. Use it when a storm engulfs the range by taking refuge in a tent or in one of the four shelters. If your week's weather turns out to be perfect, you have a day to rest and loaf at Speck Pond shelter before completing the Mahoosuc Range on Old Speck Mountain and descending to Grafton Notch, where you meet asphalt again on ME 26.

Transportation arrangements will vary to fit individual plans. You can leave your car parked near the trail at Grafton Notch and be driven around west to Shelburne. You may plan to be met at Grafton Notch on the seventh day.

Although either Shelburne or Grafton Notch could be the starting point, the northeast direction from Mount Hayes has one specific advantage. Progress northeastward gives you an exciting sense of increasing wildness. With this you also enjoy a continual, although intermittent, ascent: Mount Hayes, 2,555 feet; Mount Success, 3,565 feet; Old Speck, 4,170 feet; with 10 other summits in between.

The Mahoosuc Range has become a "laboratory" for AMC research on trail use and methods for preserving the mountain environment. First with the cooperation of the Brown Company and then with the James River Company, the AMC replaced old shelters, built tent platforms, and improved the trail with stone steps and stairs and log walkways, as well as with waterbars for erosion control. (There is a small fee for overnight stays at Speck Pond Campsite.)

The plan of this backpack takes you to shelters for five of the six nights. You will need your tent, however, at Trident Col Tentsite, and probably near the shelters if they are fully occupied when you arrive. Also,

you may require the tent for protection in an emergency, such as an injury or a severe storm. Otherwise, no camping is allowed except at authorized locations. Fires are allowed only at shelters and at Trident Col Tentsite. Backpacker stoves may be used along the trail for a hot meal and are almost a necessity at the shelters if the fireplace is in use when you want to cook. And carry a collapsible water container for trips to the springs at some of the shelters.

Concerning your outfit, I will point out that it should be as light as possible, consistent with carrying plenty of food, water, and adequate equipment. Your tent, stove, cooking utensils, sleeping bag, rain gear, clothing, and the backpack itself *must* be tested and reliable. None of them can be replaced. If you are not an experienced backpacker, I suggest that you try out both equipment and similar food on at least two shakedown trips before going on this one. Two other admonitions occur to me. One necessity always in short supply along the summits of the Mahoosucs is water. Sources are few, far between, and except at shelters, often unreliable. You'll need more water bottles than for ordinary hikes. Next, fitness. Obviously, strength and endurance for heavy backpacking are absolutely necessary to ensure both safety and enjoyment.

These comments about the demands that the Mahoosucs make on you and your outfit are meant not to discourage you but to advise on the measures you should take for a happy and rewarding backpack.

First Day: Hogan Road, Shelburne, to Mount Hayes, Cascade Mountain, and Trident Col Tentsite

Distance: 8 miles

Walking time: 6 hours

You'll want to be at the Shelburne trailhead early in the morning, perhaps from overnight accommodations nearby. The day's backpack will be long, but not overly strenuous or rugged.

HOW TO GET THERE

Drive US 2 to North Road in Shelburne. North Road's western junction with US 2 is 3.5 miles east of Gorham. (Parking for the Rattle River Trail, the route of the AT south, is about 300 yards farther east on US 2.) Turn north onto North Road and drive across the bridge over the Androscoggin River. At 0.5 mile from US 2, turn left onto Hogan Road. Drive this rough dirt road for 0.25 mile to your point of departure (parking overnight is not advised). The Centennial Trail begins on the north side of the road as a wide pathway remaining from former logging operations.

This is the last chance to check your equipment and food and water. Take an ample day's requirement of water. There may be none on the trail until Trident Col Tentsite.

THE TRAIL

The Centennial Trail was named for the AMC's 100th anniversary, when it was laid out and cut in 1976. After 150 feet along the pathway, turn left at a sign where the woods road continues straight ahead. You are on a trail now. It winds up through a hardwood forest. The white AT blazes lead you upward over stone steps past ledges on the right to the first lookoff on the left, across the lake formed by a dam in the Androscoggin bisected by the Canadian National Railroad— the former Grand Trunk. Face around and follow a short section of trail north to an old logging road, which the Centennial follows to the left. Views and occasional steps alternate with easy slabbing of the contours as you walk through beech woods. Some of the gray, smooth trunks show marks of claws dug in by bears climbing eagerly for beech-

nuts. On several ledges you'll walk over the brass plugs that identify the Appalachian National Scenic Trail.

At last, above a jumble of rock slabs, you get the first glimpses of the Mahoosucs rising ahead of you to the east. The trail curves up into open spaces among scrubby spruces to a bare knob, then on through birches to the junction among sparse evergreens at the Mahoosuc Trail from Mount Hayes and Gorham.

Here you may leave your pack and follow the Mahoosuc Trail west over the summit of Hayes to the cliffs above Gorham and the wide easterly bend of the Androscoggin south of Berlin. Away west, Mounts Madison, Adams, and Washington rise magnificently stark and barren at the summits. You look south to Pinkham Notch and the Carter-Moriah Range forming the notch's eastern slope. This side jaunt over Mount Hayes will take about 45 minutes, but is worth it on a clear day, and I've included the distance and time in the total.

Back at the junction with the Centennial Trail, shoulder your pack and head north on the Mahoosuc Trail, which is now the AT. It descends from the bare ledges, blueberry bushes, and evergreens of Mount Hayes into the leafy woods of the col between Hayes and Cascade Mountain. This col might better be described with the woodsman's term "sag" rather than the mountaineer's "col." It's a low wooded valley between the two mountains.

Next comes Cascade Mountain. The beeches and yellow and white birches change to small, parklike maples, then to bushes and broken slabs of rock. From here you'll be treated to a special sunset show. The Androscoggin River valley begins to close in with shadows. You stand far above and look across the Presidentials sharply etched by western sunlight. Move on along the ridge through spruce woods alternating

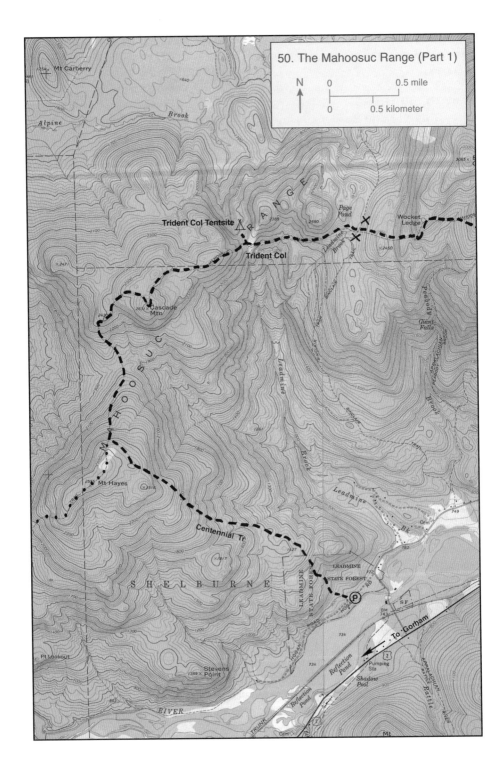

50. The Mahoosuc Range (Part 1)

N

0   0.5 mile

0   0.5 kilometer

Mt Carberry

Alpine

Brook

Trident Col Tentsite

Trident Col

RANGE

Page Pond

Wocket Ledge

Leadmine Brook

Cascade Mtn'

Peabody

Giant Falls

MAHOOSUC

Leadmine

Brook

Mt Hayes

Leadmine Bk

Cem

Centennial Tr.

SHELBURNE

LEADMINE STATE FOREST

LEADMINE STATE FOREST

P

SF

BM 743

Pt Lookout

Stevens Point

Reflection Pond

To Gorham

APPALACHIAN RATTLE RIVER

Pumping Sta

Shadow Pool

TRUNK

Reflection Pond

RIVER

Cem

Mt

with ledges and damp sphagnum moss. At the east shoulder, the Mahoosuc Trail drops steeply toward a view of distant peaks and ridges. The descent pushes your pack against your shoulders, and your hands seek steadying holds on bushes and trees, until the trail levels out at Trident Col. A spur trail leads left to water and four tentsites. This will be your camping place.

Second Day: Trident Col Tentsite to Gentian Pond Shelter

Distance: 5 miles

Walking time: 4 hours

The Mahoosuc Trail the next morning leads on eastward by an old logging road descending somewhat and slabbing south of middle Trident Peak. You cross trickles of water here and there through the hardwoods. The trail takes you up to a more recent, bulldozed road, which, after a short distance, bears right. The trail branches left, and you follow it among bushes and trees up a gradual slope to a level section. The approach to Page Pond through tall grass shows you first the spruce ridge beyond, then the oval of water. In late summer, closed gentians bloom near the beaver dam. Depending on the latest beaver work, the trail may cross over the dam's poles and mud.

An easy walk among spruces brings you to the base of the next height, Wocket Ledge, where the ridge rears up suddenly. You dig for footholds and test spruce roots and branches for secure hand grips. The ledge itself appears at the crest 50 yards to the left, about 0.75 mile from Page Pond. The climb has been strenuous, and you'll want to sit for a while and look off at the wild country near and far.

Back to the trail and up beyond the open ledge, you follow the trail in spruces. Descending, you pass a spring and the beginning of a Peabody Brook branch. Ascending and descending—the theme of the Mahoosucs—you slant down to a mountain pond called Dream Lake.

The trail turns left along the lakeshore. By stepping quietly through bushes down to the water, perhaps you see a moose feeding, belly-deep in the lake. If only lily pads and quiet ripples meet your eyes, proceed along the trail and across the inlet to the northeast end. There the Peabody Brook Trail terminates at the Mahoosuc Trail. (The Peabody Brook Trail comes up from North Road in Shelburne off US 2.) A short walk down Peabody Brook Trail takes you to a striking camera shot across Dream Lake to Mount Washington.

Returning to the Mahoosuc Trail, you head east along the inlet brook. The trail is damp, but log walkways offer dry footing. It swings left across a bog, again on walkways above the water, to a log ridge. The trail's up-and-down windings take you to a height-of-land so flat and swampy as to be almost imperceptible. The new watershed's first display appears at the boggy inlet to Moss Pond, formerly Upper Gentian Pond. You leave the shoreline for a rough, northern traverse back in the evergreens till you return to the pond near the outlet. There on your right you see a beaver dam so high that it seems barely to hold the brimming little basin from pouring down the mountainside. The dam has been doing this for many years. Two beaver lodges on the far shore house the caretakers.

The trail follows the outlet brook a short distance. Then as your way turns left, your attention will be occupied by the massive boulders it meanders among during the steep descent. A turn to the right leads you away from a cliff among white and yellow birches and swamp maples to Gentian Pond. The trail has been relocated from the west shore of Gentian Pond to its east shore; this eliminates

50. The Mahoosuc Range (Part 2)

N

0   0.5 mile

0   0.5 kilometer

a steep scramble down a ledge to a crossing of the outlet brook just below the shelter.

The shelter and its outside fireplace of piled stones rest on an abrupt, wooded dropoff, which falls away so steeply that you have a splendid view to the Androscoggin River far below in its wide valley. (From Gentian Pond Shelter, the Austin Brook Trail descends to Shelburne's North Road. Your northeast backpack in the morning will take you beyond this last trail south from the Mahoosucs.) In addition to the shelter, there are four tent platforms.

The pond water is handy and serves well enough to rinse yourself. For drinking water, you follow a faint path a good distance north among the shore spruces to an inlet trickling clear and cold past green sphagnum moss.

Third Day: Gentian Pond Shelter to Carlo Col Shelter

Distance: 5¾ miles

Walking time: 6½ hours

Mount Success is your big objective after breakfast at Gentian Pond Shelter. The climb measures the mountain's bulk rather than its height, which is a moderate 3,565 feet. The up-and-down approach makes you think that the mountain has retreated beyond ridges to fortify itself against your attack.

In early morning, a steep climb places you on ledges above the pond. Then you descend and climb again over the first of two rugged little hills protruding from the mountainside. After the second knob, a little rivulet provides a canteen filling: no more certain water until the end of the day's hike at Carlo Col Shelter.

The trail continues, steep and difficult. You surmount blocks of granite, which obstruct the way and indicate an old slide. Then you cross a washout grown to brush and begin to climb in the spruce/fir forest. The damp woods are the habitat of the deliberate spruce grouse. The trees dwindle to evergreen scrub at open ledges, and you climb toward the summit through more scrub and over bare rock.

Mount Success spreads before you northern vistas of lakes and wilderness, as well as an unusual perspective toward the Presidentials. The summit itself presents the first muddy areas typical of high Mahoosuc ridges above treeline. Lying in hollows between rock faces, the black earth has a dry crust in hot weather. Stay on the split-log walkways or you'll be into ankle-deep muck. Various heath plants border this rich humus. Matted dwarf spruces testify to the severe winds.

From Mount Success, the Mahoosuc Trail turns left down a barren shoulder into scrub and taller evergreens. The trail is rocky and at times closed in by luxuriant spruce/fir branches. Several boggy areas can be extremely wet after rain. You level out and descend into a col and junction with the Success Trail on your left. (The Success Trail is the first of five trails from the Mahoosuc Trail to the Success Pond Road, here 3 miles north. This logging road runs northeast 14 miles from Berlin to the pond.)

For the next 1.25 miles, the Mahoosuc Trail follows a northeast ridge. You climb and slab wooded contours, then descend, only to climb and descend again. In a little hollow an AT sign marks the New Hampshire–Maine line. After some rugged climbing, the trail takes you to a north outlook on bare rock surrounded by scrub and Labrador tea bushes. The view is across the vast North Country.

Now the final climb down this ledge to Carlo Col gives any backpacker pause for thought. You may wisely decide to take off your pack and lower it to a companion who has made his way down, packless, by clinging to spruces and gripping with both hands on fingerholds of rock while groping for

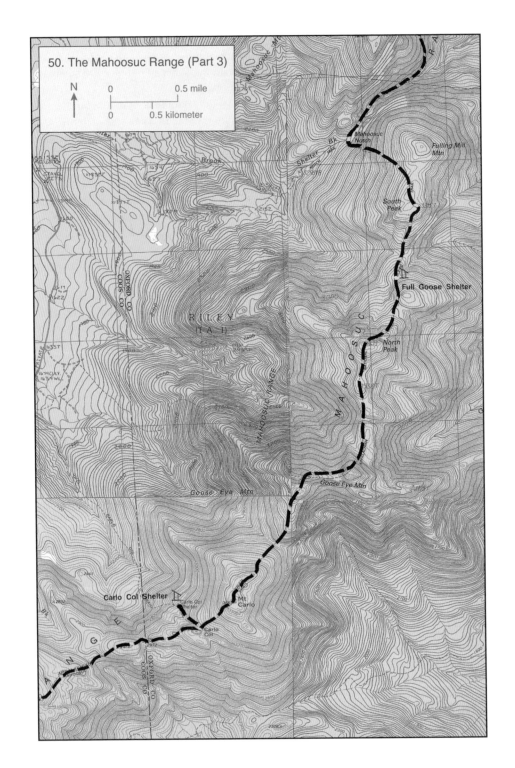

50. The Mahoosuc Range (Part 3)

N

0   0.5 mile
0   0.5 kilometer

Mahoosuc Mtn

Mahoosuc Notch

Fulling Mill Mtn

South Peak

Full Goose Shelter

RILEY (TA)

North Peak

MAHOOSUC RANGE

MAHOOSUC

Goose Eye Mtn

Goose Eye Mtn

OXFORD CO
COOS CO

Carlo Col Shelter

Carlo Col Shelter

Mt Carlo

Carlo Col

RANGE

OXFORD CO
COOS CO

footholds below. A few yards farther on, after you have reorganized yourself, you step into the deep cleft of Carlo Col. You are near your night's shelter. Turn left onto the Carlo Col Trail, and follow it down a stony 0.25 mile. At the first sign of water the trail bears left to avoid it because it has taken over the old trail. From a little ridge you descend in a wide curve to the right and return to the streamlet. Continue straight across and up a steep bank to the Carlo Col Shelter. (The Carlo Col Trail descends on the left beside the water to Success Pond Road 2.5 miles away.) The Carlo Col Shelter is built of logs like the Gentian Pond Shelter. There are five tent platforms.

Fourth Day: Carlo Col Shelter to Full Goose Shelter

Distance: 4½ miles

Walking time: 4 hours

This day's hike features Goose Eye Mountain and barren ridges such as you might see in Labrador. It begins with a starting climb from Carlo Col Shelter back to the Mahoosuc Trail. You'll feel the morning coolness because the shelter's elevation is 3,000 feet. Turn left from the Carlo Col Trail onto the Mahoosuc Trail. Mount Carlo, elevation 3,565, rises ahead, and the trail leads up through spruces. But the climb warms you before you emerge on Mount Carlo's bare summit, perhaps hidden in morning mist. You've been climbing 45 minutes if you start your day sensibly, without straining, so clearing skies and valleys may reveal the northern panorama of Success Pond and the mountains you saw yesterday afternoon before Carlo Col.

Beyond the summit, the trail crosses a bog on split-log walkways, descends into spruce woods, then goes up a ledge and down again, often through more black mud or above it on walkways. You come out onto a barren slope, which if horizontal and near the Arctic Circle could be called tundra. Your eyes are at once attracted to Goose Eye Mountain—ahead across a deep col—a distant pinnacle of rock.

Legend gives this mountain the early name of "Goose High," because the summit was an obstacle to migrating geese. The geese had to clear by a few wingbeats a rocky 3,870-foot mass.

The descent from the barrens into evergreens becomes so steep and rough that you grab at spruces to help you swing down. Don't forget to test before entrusting serious weight and balance to a tree. As you approach the transition to the col, you may find water trickling across the trail from a spring on the left. The walk across the col beside wide patches of sphagnum moss near the spruces will take you only five minutes. Then Goose Eye Mountain!

You can test your leg muscles on the stone steps, which offer steady climbing. The steepness eases at a swing left, then up you go again. Goose Eye Mountain shows you how to climb (with the aid of AT trail crew work) 500 feet in 0.25 mile.

There are more walkways, leading to more stone steps, which bear right to avoid a chimney in the mountainside. At the upper end of the stone steps, carefully climb to the log stairs. You emerge on a less demanding section, which takes you to open views over low scrub and ledges. Ahead, Goose Eye's pinnacle appears clearly. There's a last scramble in the scrub, and you top out on the east shoulder of the mountain at treeline.

The Mahoosuc Trail turns sharply right. Branching left, the Goose Eye Trail leads over the summit rocks. (And down to the Success Pond Road.) You'll want to dump your pack at the junction and climb the 200 yards to Goose Eye's peak for a rest, a snack, and the views.

Return to your pack and continue east on the Mahoosuc Trail. You walk along a rocky ridge, bare except for scattered small spruces, and you can see your next climb—East Peak. But first you traverse a section of evergreens to a col, then ascend to the bare summit. On it there's a left turn, north, down from East Peak. Watch for cairns. The trail descends across a great sloping barrens, toward the eastern corner of spruces. The seemingly subarctic flora and shrubs along the trail are so low you look off to your next destination, North Peak, and in the distance to northern forests and lakes.

You enter the scrub you've been approaching. The trail drops to the col before North Peak. The woods open up among larger spruces. At a damp, wooded ravine, you come upon small pools of water cupped in sphagnum moss.

North Peak is steep, too. The wide barrens resemble treeline areas in the Presidentials and Franconias, although here vegetation extends to the highest ground. Much of the rock is crumbly and soft. Gravel in the trail crunches under your boots.

Clouds and rain often settle over the range, and winds are icy. If you must brave a drenching exposure on a ridge such as Goose Eye's North Peak, you face subarctic winds and temperatures.

From North Peak, the Mahoosuc Trail continues east along open ground beyond the summit. You follow and descend through scrub and barrens into spruces. You find yourself walking down over ledges among older trees. Another mountain looms before you. The trail seems to vanish, however, at a wall of brush, and you are hemmed in by a ledge on your right. In years past, hikers had to pull themselves up the ledge. But now there is a small log ladder.

When you climb the ladder to the top of the ledge, you discover Full Goose Shelter. It opens toward Fulling Mill Mountain and the precipitous valleys of Bull Branch and Goose Eye Brook. Beyond are the mountains that rise above and conceal Grafton Notch.

There are four tent platforms as well as this shelter. To get a drink of water, walk past the front and take the steep path down to the spring.

Fifth Day: Full Goose Shelter to Speck Pond Shelter

Distance: 5 miles
Walking time: 7 hours

The Mahoosuc Trail continues north from Full Goose Shelter by dropping down the overlook in front of the shelter to a ravine that is only an infinitesimal hint of the Mahoosuc Notch to come. But first, the south peak of Fulling Mill Mountain. You climb up a steady grade through evergreens and reach a meadow between two wooded summits. The trail turns left, and you rapidly descend, in trees again, 1,000 feet to the western end of Mahoosuc Notch. (At a junction, left, the Notch Trail comes in from the Success Pond Road.)

You turn sharply right and follow the Mahoosuc Trail down a pleasant slope among spruces at 2,500 feet elevation. You are entering Mahoosuc Notch. The gentle approach leaves you unprepared for the gigantic rock slabs and chunks, which seem to have fallen from the high cliffs on either side. But they have not fallen recently; they are draped with moss and crusted with lichens.

The moss forms treacherous pads over crevices and caves. Be careful not to step on any moss that reaches from slab to slab. As you crawl under overhanging rocks, you hear water trickling deep down in caves. Winter chill comes to you from the ice caverns. You follow white paint marks as the trail twists and turns for a mile among the rocks. You should plan on needing at least two hours, during which you'll be busy reaching for

50. The Mahoosuc Range (Part 4)

N

0   0.5 mile

0   0.5 kilometer

The Eyebrow

Grafton Notch

Table Rock

Moose Cave

GRAFTON NOTCH STATE PARK

G R A F T O N

(T A 2)

Old Speck Mtn

4180

Speck Pond Shelter

Speck Pond

Mahoosuc Arm

Pond

Brook

Notch 2

R A N G E

Mahoosuc Mtn

Silver

Stream

Mahoosuc Notch

Shelter

Fulling Mill Mtn

Bull

Riley Hill

South Peak

⛺ Full Goose Shelter

R I L E Y

handholds, stepping wide, balancing, and creeping.

At the notch's eastern end, you resume normal woods hiking. The trail follows the brook past the site of a former small beaver pond. Below this, after entering big hardwoods, you turn left away from the brook, climb up a short distance, and bear right onto an old logging road. In a slabbing ascent, the trail rounds Mahoosuc Mountain.

The trail follows a logging road toward a sag known as Notch 2 until you cross a brook. After a rough section, you begin the day's second real climb as the trail swings up Mahoosuc Arm. Much of the way, the trail rises among tall, old spruces. Mahoosuc Arm extends 1,200 feet above Mahoosuc Notch.

About halfway, or 0.75 mile from the notch, you come to a seasonal brook in a rock sluice; don't count on water.

Climbing on, you enter evergreen scrub and begin to ascend sloping ledges. The trail follows cairns along rock worn by glaciers and ages of weathering. You come out on the bare ridge itself, Mahoosuc Arm, which is really a mountain almost 3,800 feet high.

A big cairn and post on the open ledges mark the summit of Mahoosuc Arm. Here the Mahoosuc Trail turns right. (The May Cutoff, a cutoff trail to Speck Pond Trail, forks left.) The Mahoosuc Trail jogs approximately south and then north along the ridge and enters occasional scrub between open meadows. Now going down more steeply through

View from Mount Success

ROBERT J. KOZLOW

Backpacking Hikes

spruce woods, you descend to 3,500 feet and Speck Pond. The trail circles to the east shore, and at the upper end you come to Speck Pond Campsite, which includes the shelter and six tent platforms. In the summer, this campsite has a caretaker, and there is a fee for overnight camping.

A small, deep mountain lake, Speck Pond is the highest in Maine, and has been measured 50 feet to the bottom. Beavers may raise the depth at times with a dam in the outlet, which is Pond Brook. The pond reflects the surrounding pointed spruces, or sometimes, due to its elevation, lies smothered in clouds. (The Speck Pond Trail leaves from the shelter for the Success Pond Road.)

Sixth Day
Allowed for bad weather or to spend at Speck Pond.

Seventh Day: Speck Pond Shelter to Grafton Notch
Distance: 4¾ miles
Walking time: 4½ hours
Your departure in the morning should be adjusted to the weather. Foggy daylight and gloomy spruce woods have been known to brighten in an hour, and too-eager hikers have arrived at Old Speck's summit to find it shrouded in clouds, and by quickly descending to Grafton Notch have missed the spectacular scenery spread out in all directions from the observation tower. Now that you have been conditioned by the Mahoosucs, you should be able to climb Old Speck and descend to Grafton Notch in 4.5 hours. So wait a while for clear skies.

Take the Mahoosuc Trail from Speck Pond Campsite northeast. Directly, it climbs up a large knoll, drops down, and then up and around another ridge. In the next little valley, you pass a spring east of the trail. You begin to climb up Old Speck along ledges that lead you on upward at the apex of their angles, which drop off on either side.

This rocky shoulder joins spruce woods, and the trail, bearing right, leads into them. The trail parallels for a time the blue paint blazes identifying the boundary of Grafton Notch State Park. You are nearing the highest elevation of your backpack week—4,180 feet. As you approach the summit of Old Speck, you pass on your left the Old Speck Trail to Grafton Notch and the highway, ME 26. This trail will be the route of your descent. From this junction to the summit, a little over 0.25 mile, you may as well carry your pack along the more level section to the clearing in the evergreens surrounding the observation tower.

The view northward is toward Umbagog Lake and the Rangeley Lakes, whose waters shine like mirrors on a sunny day. To the southwest, the peaks, ravines, and barren heaths of the rugged range you've climbed over stretch away to the Presidentials.

From the summit clearing, retrace your steps along the Mahoosuc Trail to the Old Speck Trail. Turn right onto the Old Speck Trail for your 3.5-mile downward loop to the depths of Grafton Notch. First the trail takes you steeply down to a long northern ridge. As you begin this, the trail turns northwest and the Link Trail enters on your right. (Now closed, the Link Trail gave steep access to the site of the former cabin for the fire warden.)

Walk past the Link Trail along the northern ridge for about 0.5 mile. You'll be descending with a steady, sometimes rough, loss of altitude in the spruce/fir forest. The trail swings eastward among tall spruces and leaves the ridge at an outlook into the notch and down the Bear River valley to Newry, and across the notch, to nearby Baldpate Mountain. The Eyebrow Trail comes in on your left. (The Eyebrow Trail traverses the upper edge of an 800-foot cliff called The Eyebrow and is not for backpackers.) Climb down to the right of the Eyebrow Trail junction on the Old Speck Trail. Stone steps, waterbars, and log steps will assist you for the remaining mile of this section, which has almost literally been attached to the mountainside by trail crews.

You cross a small stream, the head of Cascade Brook. The trail turns left and follows the south edge of the rock that carries the cascades. Then a right turn puts you on more log steps leading down into yellow birches and beeches. These deciduous trees indicate you've come down to a milder climate. The trail follows a series of switchbacks.

Grafton Notch is so narrow that you have scarcely 100 yards—after you pass the lower Eyebrow Trail entering on your left—of level walking till you reach a kiosk and step out onto the large parking area for the Grafton Notch State Park. (From the kiosk, the AT continues east across ME 26 to climb over Baldpate Mountain on its way to Katahdin.)

Now you are back in the world of wheeled transportation for the first time in a week.

There is a major flaw in my character, to wit: I take serious subjects lightly, and light subjects seriously. Brooks are considered ordinarily nothing but light subjects. They are suitable for light lyrical verse, for instance. They have been a serious part of my life.

Thus too with the love of Nature. The subject of Nature only becomes serious when it is subjected to scientific inquiry.

Thus also with taking care of Nature or, to use its real meaning, taking care of our world.

This serious subject I take lightly. I suggest that the infrastructure of environmentalism—how I like this modern jargon!—is very simple. The basis for looking after our planet is birth control. Margaret Sanger laid out the solution years ago. Earth Day celebrants should place statues of her in every park and parade in her memory.

—Daniel Doan, "Notes"